New Heinemann Maths

Textbook

Heinemann

Heinemann is an imprint of Pearson Education Limited, a company incorporated in England and Wales, having its registered office at Edinburgh Gate, Harlow, Essex, CM20 2JE.
Registered company number: 872828

Heinemann is a registered trademark of Pearson Education Limited

Writing team
John T Blair
Percy W Farren
Myra A Pearson
John W Thayers
David K Thomson

First published 2001

11
16

ISBN 978 0 435174 22 4

Produced by Gecko Ltd.
Illustrated by Tessa Richardson-Jones, Shelagh McNicholas, Debbie Clark, Teri Gower, David Till.
Printed and bound in China (CTPS/16)

Contents

SAVINGS BANK

Write the amount

1 ten pounds more than

   (a) £370   **(b)** £807   **(c)** £690   **(d)** £96

2 ten pounds less than

   (a) £750   **(b)** £413   **(c)** £108   **(d)** £900

3 one hundred pounds more than

   (a) £259   **(b)** £701   **(c)** £640   **(d)** £900

4 one hundred pounds less than

   (a) £809   **(b)** £445   **(c)** £780   **(d)** £162

5 fifty pounds more than

   (a) £600   **(b)** £150   **(c)** £450   **(d)** £950

6 fifty pounds less than

   (a) £850   **(b)** £400   **(c)** £700   **(d)** £150.

Tom	Pat	Kim	Roy	Ben	Ann
£210	£300	£50	£101	£95	£305

7 How much money does each person have after

   (a) Pat gives Kim £50   **(b)** Ann gives Roy £100

   (c) Tom gives Ben £10?

8 Write the multiple

   (a) of 10 between 370 and 390

   (b) of 100 between 800 and 600

   (c) of 50 between 400 and 500.

1 Write the number

(a) after 3682   (b) before 5001

(c) 1 more than 3999   (d) 1 less than 4080

(e) 2 more than 6300   (f) 2 less than 2000.

2 List the numbers between

(a) 3417 and 3421   (b) 6403 and 6398

(c) 8996 and 9003   (d) 1004 and 995.

3 Write the number

• 10 more than   (a) 1560   (b) 7000   (c) 6590   (d) 4993

• 10 less than   (e) 5270   (f) 2600   (g) 3031   (h) 10000.

4 Find the length of each bridge.

(a)

(b)

10 m longer than 1328 m   10 m shorter than 1006 m

5 Write **the** multiple of 10 between

(a) 2170 and 2190   (b) 10000 and 9980 (c) 6990 and 7010.

6 Write **a** multiple of 10 between

(a) 7000 and 7100   (b) 9050 and 9000   (c) 3050 and 2950.

3

1 Write each computer game score.

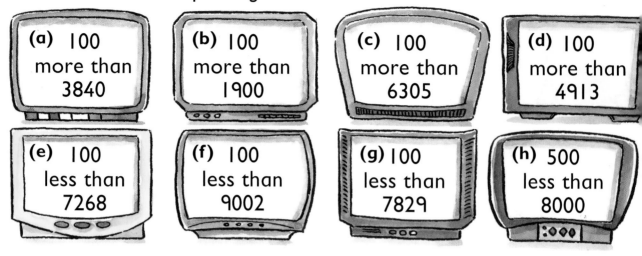

(a) 100 more than 3840

(b) 100 more than 1900

(c) 100 more than 6305

(d) 100 more than 4913

(e) 100 less than 7268

(f) 100 less than 9002

(g) 100 less than 7829

(h) 500 less than 8000

2 Write the number
- 1000 more than   (a) 2100   (b) 4630   (c) 8307   (d) 424
- 1000 less than   (e) 5700   (f) 4409   (g) 9000   (h) 1520.

3 How many points does each player have now?

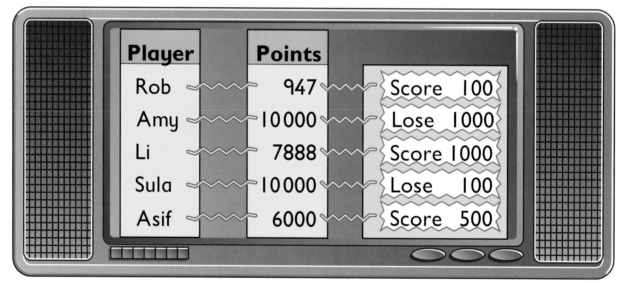

Player	Points	
Rob	947	Score 100
Amy	10000	Lose 1000
Li	7888	Score 1000
Sula	10000	Lose 100
Asif	6000	Score 500

4 Write a multiple of 100 between
(a) 9300 and 9500   (b) 7000 and 6000   (c) 4100 and 3900.

5 Write a multiple of 1000 between
(a) 4000 and 2000   (b) 10000 and 6000   (c) 3000 and 0.

1 Write the number which has

(a) 5 units
(b) 7 tens
(c) 9 hundreds
(d) 6 thousands
(e) 0 units
(f) 2 hundreds
(g) 0 tens
(h) 1 thousand
(i) 1 hundred.

2 Write the number with

(a) thousands digit 3 **and** hundreds digit 1
(b) hundreds digit 5 **and** units digit 7
(c) thousands digit 3 **and** tens digit 1
(d) hundreds **and** tens digits 0.

3

What is my number?

- The thousands digit is 8, which is two more than the hundreds digit.
- The units digit is one less than the tens digit.
- The hundreds digit is double the units digit.

5

1 **Add 10**

397 → (a)

4008 → (b)

7256 → (c)

2 **Add 100**

725 → (a)

930 → (b)

5000 → (c)

3 **Add 1000**

342 → (a)

1050 → (b)

6001 → (c)

4 **Subtract 10**

2350 → (a)

7010 → (b)

1002 → (c)

5 **Subtract 100**

3781 → (a)

1099 → (b)

4003 → (c)

6 **Subtract 1000**

1547 → (a)

7700 → (b)

10000 → (c)

7

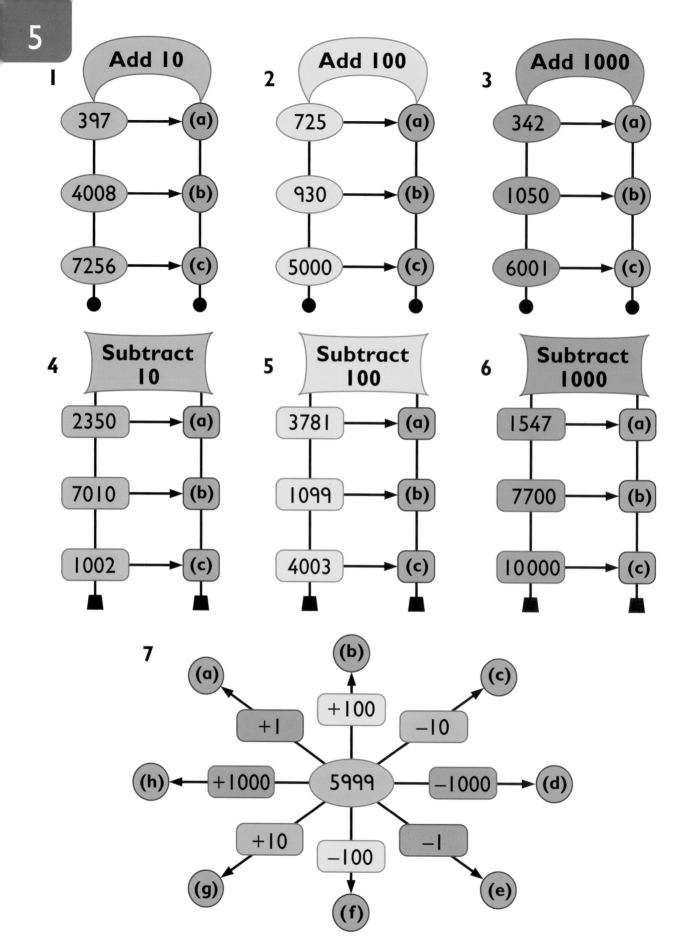

5999

+1 → (a)

+100 → (b)

−10 → (c)

+1000 → (h)

−1000 → (d)

+10 → (g)

−100 → (f)

−1 → (e)

1 Write the **larger** number.

(a) 3756 4032   (b) 5900 5099   (c) 7236 7362

2 Write the **smaller** number.

(a) 4189 4201   (b) 1001 987   (c) 5110 5010

3 Write **true** or **false** for each example.

(a) 6087 > 5987   (b) 3060 < 3606   (c) 2717 < 2171

(d) 10000 > 9100   (e) 2002 > 2220   (f) 9600 < 9660

4 Write the **(a) largest** amount   **(b) smallest** amount.

£6180   £6080   £6810   £6101   £6800

5 What colour is the **(a)** cheapest car **(b)** most expensive car?

£9052   £9526   £9265   £9605   £9562   £9650

6 Write in order. Start with

(a) the **heaviest**

1908 kg   2001 kg   1809 kg   2110 kg   1098 kg

(b) the **lightest**.

3645 kg   4654 kg   3465 kg   4546 kg   3546 kg

I Write using **numerals**.

(a) Ten thousand.

(b) Two thousand five hundred.

(c) Five thousand two hundred and fifty.

(d) Nine thousand and thirty-two.

(e) Three thousand four hundred and seventeen.

(f) Seven thousand and one.

2 Write in **words**.

(a) 4000

(b) 1007

(c) 8300

(d) 6623

7 3 8 6

3 Write **in words** using **all four digits**

(a) the largest possible number   (b) the smallest possible numbe

1 Who is reading the

(a) 80th page   (b) 90th page   (c) 70th page

(d) 60th page   (e) 50th page   (f) 100th page?

2 Who has read   (a) most pages   (b) fewest pages?

3 Who has read

(a) 10 more pages than Sam

(b) 20 more pages than Mia

(c) double Sue's number of pages?

4 Write in **words**.

(a) 40th   (b) 10th   (c) 100th   (d) 30th   (e) 20th

Estimate.

1 About how many **centimetres** has each snail travelled?

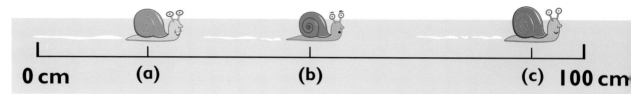

0 cm   (a)   (b)   (c) 100 cm

2 About how many **metres** has each runner travelled?

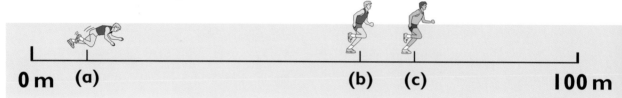

0 m   (a)   (b)   (c)   100 m

3 About how many **kilometres** has each car travelled?

0 km   (a)   (b)   (c)   100 km

4 The number on each lid shows how many sweets
the jar holds when full.
About how many sweets are in each jar now?

(a)   (b)   (c)

50 fizzers   100 chews   1000 mints

1 How many people, to the **nearest hundred**, live in each of these villages?

(a)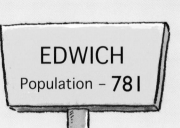
EDWICH
Population – 781

(b)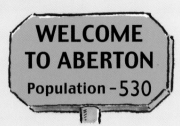
WELCOME TO ABERTON
Population – 530

(c)
OAKHAM
Population – 973

2 Write to the **nearest hundred**.

(a) 449   (b) 98   (c) 707   (d) 991   (e) 350

3 List the numbers

(a) nearer to 70 than 80

| 77 | 74 | 71 | 79 | 75 |

(b) nearer to 730 than 720.

| 728 | 722 | 725 | 723 | 726 |

4 Write the height of each mountain to the **nearest ten** metres.

(a) Snowpeak   (b) Ben Rory   (c) Mount Erin

848 m   662 m   535 m

5 Write to the **nearest ten**.

(a) 119   (b) 751   (c) 604   (d) 555   (e) 997

6 Write each distance from Farnham

(a) to the **nearest hundred** miles

(b) to the **nearest ten** miles.

Distances from Farnham	
Edwich	–	86 miles
Aberton	–	264 miles
Oakham	–	225 miles

Double each number

1

(a) 12	(b) 24	(c) 33	(d) 42	(e) 13
(f) 41	(g) 32	(h) 14	(i) 22	(j) 34
(k) 21	(l) 44	(m) 23	(n) 31	(o) 11

2 Write each number from a red card with its double from a blue card.

27 48 28 47   Double   96 78 54 58

16 39 29   32 94 56

3

(a) 43 + 43	(b) 43 + 44	(c) 42 + 43
(d) 36 + 36	(e) 36 + 34	(f) 38 + 36

4
(a) 17 + 19   (b) 37 + 35   (c) 47 + 48   (d) 26 + 27

(e) 38 + 39   (f) 46 + 45   (g) 27 + 25   (h) 16 + 18

(i) 22 + 23   (j) 35 + 34   (k) 13 + 15   (l) 44 + 46

1 How many pieces of litter altogether did each child collect?

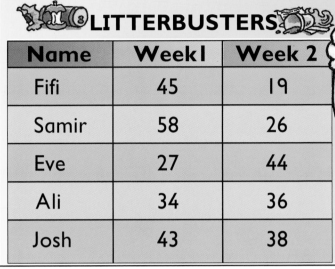

LITTERBUSTERS		
Name	Week1	Week 2
Fifi	45	19
Samir	58	26
Eve	27	44
Ali	34	36
Josh	43	38

2

Suzi — 38 cans

Jake — 26 cans

Becky — 47 cans

Zoe — 59 cans

Cal — 35 cans

Find the total number of cans collected by

(a) Suzi and Becky (b) Zoe and Jake (c) Jake and Cal

(d) Becky and Cal (e) Jake and Becky (f) Suzi and Zoe.

3 How many cans does each child still need to collect to reach the target?

LITTER BUSTERS TARGET 100 CANS

4 (a) 58 + ■ = 73 (b) 27 + ■ = 81 (c) 38 + ■ = 96

(d) ■ + 17 = 94 (e) ■ + 46 = 93 (f) ■ + 24 = 92

1 How many points altogether were scored by the

- red player
- green player
- yellow player
- blue player
- black player
- white player?

2 Each player threw another ball to give these new totals.

red ⟶ 50 points   yellow ➤ 41 points   black ➤ 54 points

green ➤53 points   blue ⟶ 49 points   white ➤ 68 points

Which number did each player hit?

3 List different ways of scoring 30 with **three** throws.

1 How much money does each person have?

I have £40 more than Zac.

Mae

I have £19.

Molly

I have double the amount Molly has.

Zac

I have £22 more than Mae.

Tara

I have £26 more than Molly and Zac together.

Jack

2 Find each child's number.

The total of 12, 14, 8, 15 and 10.

Wasim

The sum of 16 and 17 added to 48.

Sue

When I add 48 to my number, the total is 75.

Ann

28 added to double the sum of 13 and 15.

Des

| 48 | 55 | 26 | 33 |
| 27 | 45 | 38 | 46 |

3 Write two numbers which

(a) total between 60 and 70

(b) are even and have a sum between 80 and 90

(c) are odd and have a total greater than 90.

 70p  48p  60p  57p

1 Find the total cost of

(a) and

(b)  and

(c) and

(d) and

2 (a) 84 + 50   (b) 65 + 80   (c) 90 + 74

   (d) 20 + 96   (e) 90 + 16   (f) 83 + 40

   (g) 98 + 30   (h) 50 + 72   (i) 80 + 71

3  80 cards   72 cards   How many cards altogether?

 47   90    83   50

4 (a) Who has more balloons?

   (b) How many more?

                       Alex   Sarah

5 Tom has 40 red balloons, 85 blue balloons and 30 yellow balloons. How many does he have altogether?

6 (a) 63 + ■ = 133   (b) 50 + ■ = 148   (c) 85 + ■ = 165

   (d) ■ + 40 = 127   (e) ■ + 72 = 102   (f) ■ + 90 = 189

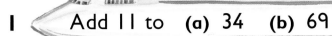

1 Add 11 to **(a)** 34 **(b)** 69 **(c)** 93

2 Add 9 to **(a)** 48 **(b)** 75 **(c)** 96

3

(a) 56 + 30	**(b)** 56 + 31	**(c)** 56 + 29
(d) 50 + 84	**(e)** 51 + 84	**(f)** 49 + 84

4 Write each total.

(a)  68 41

(b)  69 53

(c)  75 61

(d)  63 39

5 **(a)** 95 + 21 **(b)** 79 + 33 **(c)** 46 + 71
(d) 34 + 82 **(e)** 86 + 48 **(f)** 62 + 57

6 How many passengers flew to

(a) London

(b) Paris

(c) Aberdeen

(d) Birmingham?

	Number of passengers	
	Adults	**Children**
London	84	49
Paris	73	41
Aberdeen	82	26
Birmingham	91	58

67 42 74 85

1 How many passengers altogether are on
   (a) the green and red buses   (b) the blue and yellow buses
   (c) the yellow and green buses   (d) the green and blue buses?

2 (a) 54 + 62   (b) 73 + 95   (c) 36 + 83
   (d) 77 + 44   (e) 65 + 76   (f) 57 + 48

3 Find the total cost of each pair of tickets.

(a)   (b)   (c)

46p 76p   65p 88p   74p 57p

4

Ayton School	Byford School	Cardale School	Didley School
63	59	74	48

Which two schools will fill **exactly**

(a) the brown bus

(b) the white bus?

 holds 137

 holds 111

5 (a) 43 + ■ = 126   (b) 57 + ■ = 139   BUS STOP
   (c) 85 + ■ = 113   (d) 49 + ■ = 124

1 Add the amounts in bags of the same colour.

£240 £120 £430 £620 £850

£70 £20 £30 £40 £80

2 What is the total amount in each safe?

(a) £435 / £50

(b) £309 / £70

(c) £819 / £80

(d) £40 / £545

3

(a) £340 + £■ = £390

(b) £■ + £425 = £445

(c) £363 + £■ = £393

4

(a) 416 + 20 (b) 416 + 19

(c) 444 + 29 (d) 623 + 39

(e) 546 + 9 (f) 705 + 69

(g) 364 + 18 (h) 866 + 28

(i) 305 + 57 (j) 414 + 77

5

(a) 353 + 40 (b) 353 + 41

(c) 666 + 31 (d) 507 + 51

(e) 258 + 11 (f) 715 + 41

(g) 224 + 22 (h) 532 + 62

(i) 818 + 83 (j) 931 + 63

Cash box £££

£180 £60 £420 £50 £350
£560 £90
£240 £70 £40 £80 £70

1 Add the amounts on the

(a) green envelopes (b) blue envelopes (c) red envelopes

(d) yellow envelopes (e) white envelopes (f) brown envelopes

2 What is the total amount in each pair of money bags?

(a) £775 £40 (b) £462 £70 (c) £534 £90

(d) £81 £30 (e) £854 £60 (f) £322 £80

(g) £70 £195 (h) £645 £90 (i) £96 £50

3

(a) 370 + ■ = 440   (b) ■ + 160 = 230   (c) 650 + ■ = 690

(d) 586 + ■ = 626   (e) ■ + 183 = 203   (f) 829 + ■ = 919

1 Double each number.

(a) 140
(b) 430
(c) 340
(d) 220
(e) 310

2 Write each number from the red shirt with its double from the green shirt.

480	60
170	380
90	260

520	340
120	180
960	760

3

(a) 320 + 320

(b) 320 + 330

(c) 310 + 320

(d) 160 + 160

(e) 170 + 160

(f) 160 + 180

(g) 280 + 280

(h) 280 + 290

(i) 270 + 280

4

(a) 220 + 230

(b) 130 + 140

(c) 290 + 310

(d) 360 + 370

(e) 480 + 470

(f) 340 + 360

(g) 270 + 290

(h) 180 + 160

1 What number from the machine is added to

(a) 170 to make 200

(b) 440 to make 500

(c) 865 to make 900

(d) 572 to make 600

(e) 284 to make 300

(f) 309 to make 400?

2 How many more are needed to fill each box?

(a)

426 holds 500

(b)

262 holds 300

3 How many more are needed to fill each jar?

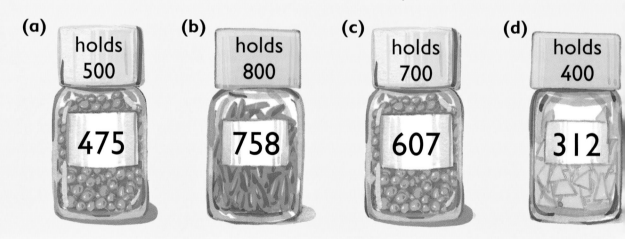

(a) holds 500 — 475

(b) holds 800 — 758

(c) holds 700 — 607

(d) holds 400 — 312

4 (a) $110 + \blacksquare = 200$ (b) $560 + \blacksquare = 600$ (c) $819 + \blacksquare = 900$

(d) $\blacksquare + 668 = 700$ (e) $\blacksquare + 721 = 800$ (f) $\blacksquare + 985 = 1000$

1 Which door does each key open?

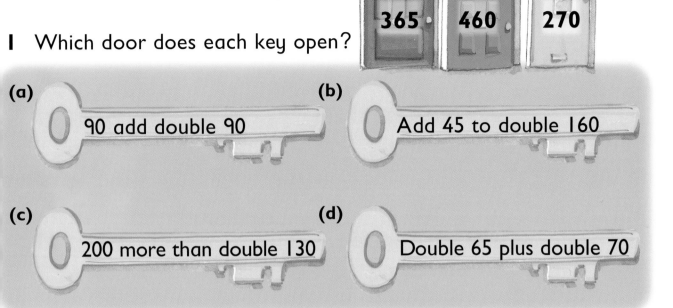

365 **460** **270**

(a) 90 add double 90

(b) Add 45 to double 160

(c) 200 more than double 130

(d) Double 65 plus double 70

2 Use **four** of the numbers to make the addition story true.

37 59 64 71 93   ■ + ▲ = ○ + ◆

3

180 80 260 390 270

jug holds 260 tub holds 530

Which **two** colours together fill **exactly**

(a) the jug   (b) the tub?

4 How many more 🫐 are needed to fill the pot?

300 253

pot holds 600

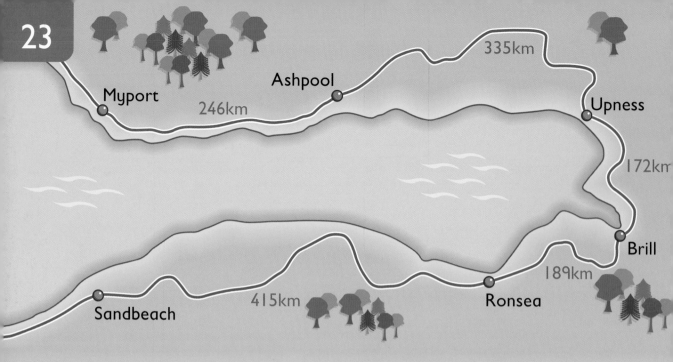

1 What is the distance by road between

   (a) Myport and Upness   (b) Ashpool and Brill

   (c) Upness and Ronsea   (d) Brill and Sandbeach?

2 How many kilometres are there in a **return** journey between

   (a) Myport and Ashpool   (b) Brill and Ronsea?

3 (a) 557 + 434   (b) 173 + 660   (c) 258 + 476

   (d) 397 + 545   (e) 558 + 289   (f) 679 + 273

   (g) 765 + 135   (h) 209 + 296   (i) 144 + 586

4

My house is between Ashpool and Upness.
It is 176 km from Ashpool and 159 km from Upness.

How far is Ryan's house from

   (a) Myport   (b) Brill?

Ryan

School Fund-Raising Week

1 Which table tennis team raised

   (a) most money   **(b)** least money?

Class 4
Table tennis marathon

Red team		Blue team		Green team		Purple team	
Lee	£239	Cara	£183	Greg	£158	Emma	£75
Phil	£162	Zoe	£217	Sally	£245	Raja	£327

2 Find the total amount of money raised by each of these events.

   (a)   **(b)**

Class 4
Sponsored Swim

Name	Amount
Mandy	£249
Bill	£217
Ros	£235
Rashmi	£172
Paul	£88

Class 4
Sponsored Cycle

Name	Amount
Anwar	£206
Mark	£187
Kim	£92
Jo	£265
Sam	£250

3 Which two children raised a total of

   (a) exactly £180   **(b)** exactly £500?

4 Which of the three **events** raised

   (a) the greatest amount   **(b)** the least amount?

1 How many plants are left?
(a) Sell 21.

(b) Sell 19.

56

44

2

(a) 92 – 41　　　(b) 85 – 71　　　(c) 73 – 49
(d) Subtract 69 from 97.　　　(e) 60 take away 29

3 How many plants are left?
(a) Sell 22.

(b) Sell 22.

38

87

(c) Sell 18.

(d) Sell 18.

35

53

4

(a) 74 – 32　　　(b) 86 – 52　　　(c) 95 – 68
(d) Take 58 from 77.　　　(e) 94 minus 78

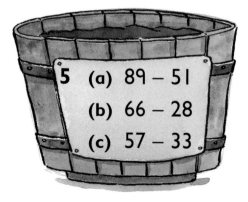

5 (a) 89 – 51
(b) 66 – 28
(c) 57 – 33

6 (a) 70 – 52
(b) 63 – 39
(c) 84 – 37

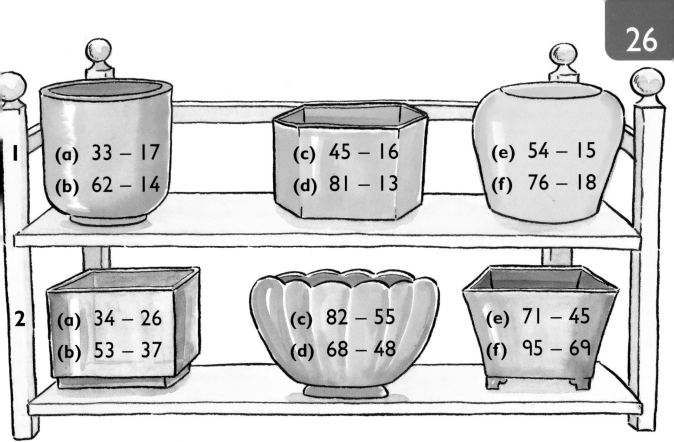

1
(a) 33 – 17
(b) 62 – 14
(c) 45 – 16
(d) 81 – 13
(e) 54 – 15
(f) 76 – 18

2
(a) 34 – 26
(b) 53 – 37
(c) 82 – 55
(d) 68 – 48
(e) 71 – 45
(f) 95 – 69

3 Find the difference in price between the

(a) green and yellow pots

(b) brown and green pots

(c) brown and yellow pots

(d) red and green pots.

£43

£92

£60

£84

4 How much more does the dearest pot cost than the cheapest?

5 The price of each pot is reduced by £15.
What is the new price of each pot?

6 (a) 76 – ■ = 48   (b) 55 – ■ = 28   (c) 64 – ■ = 26

1 Copy and complete each child's work.

Anna
32 + 25 =
25 + 32 =
57 − 32 =
57 − 25 =

Ben
62 − 34 =
62 − 28 =
34 + 28 =
▢ + 34 =

Chan
26 + 47 =
47 + ▢ =
73 − ▢ =
▢ − 47 =

2 Write 2 addition stories **and** 2 subtraction stories using each set of three numbers.

43 27 16
Anna

92 37 55
Ben

19 77 58
Chan

48 37 85
Dee

3 (a) Who has subtracted correctly? Check by **adding**.

Anna
33 − 17 = 16

Ben
72 − 27 = 35

Chan
65 − 29 = 36

(b) For each **correct** subtraction, write

• the addition you used to check

• another addition you **could** use to check.

1 Which of these room numbers are **(a)** even **(b)** odd?

56 84 95 53 32 71 60 17 38 24

2 Find the difference between the numbers on these discs.

(a) red and orange   (b) brown and yellow

(c) blue and yellow   (d) orange and blue

(e) red and green   (f) brown and red

84 56 32
24 60 38

3 (a) What kind of number is each answer in question **2**?

(b) What do you notice when you find the difference between two **even** numbers?

4 Find the difference between the numbers on these discs.

(a) orange and green   (b) blue and yellow

(c) yellow and brown   (d) brown and orange

(e) yellow and green   (f) red and blue

53 95 67
71 17 35

5 (a) What kind of number is each answer in question **4**?

(b) What do you notice when you find the difference between two **odd** numbers?

6 Investigate. What do you notice when you find the difference between an odd and an even number?

1 How much does each have left?

(a)  £106

Give £7 to **Petcare**.

(b)  £103

Give £4.

(c) £102

Give £6.

(d)  £101

Give £5.

(e) £104

Give £9.

2 (a) 300 – 7   (b) 605 – 6   (c) 502 – 4

(d) 701 – 8   (e) 207 – 9   (f) 904 – 6

(g) 906 – ■ = 897   (h) 803 – ■ = 798   (i) 408 – ■ = 399

3 How much does each have left?

(a)  £134

Give £7 to **Childhelp**.

(b)  £126

Give £8.

(c)  £152

Give £9.

(d)  £183

Give £5.

(e)  £141

Give £4.

(f)  £175

Give £8.

4 (a) Subtract 7 from 323.   (b) Take 9 from 545.

(c) 215 minus 7   (d) 652 subtract 7

(e) 5 less than 730   (f) 461 take away 3

1 How many are left when these are sold?

   (a) 80 books   (b) 90 postcards   (c) 60 comics

   (d) 80 toys   (e) 40 buttons   (f) 70 CDs

2 (a) 132 – 40   (b) 175 – 90   (c) 121 – 30

   (d) 144 – 80   (e) 113 – 70   (f) 158 – 60

   (g) 166 – ■ = 86   (h) 110 – ■ = 60   (i) 127 – ■ = 67

3 Find the difference between

(a)

143 and 61

(b)

126 and 89

(c)

134 and 69

(d)

128 and 41

4 (a) 18 less than 111   (b) Take 12 from 105.

   (c) 117 minus 23   (d) 108 subtract 27

   (e) Subtract 38 from 125. (f) 127 take away 32

5 Find 6 pairs of numbers between 60 and 140 with a
   difference of 49.

SCOREBOARD	red	blue	yellow	green
1st round	381	300	281	200
2nd round	360	280	290	140
3rd round	■	310	■	■

1 Find the difference between the **first round** scores of the

(a) blues and greens   (b) reds and yellows

(c) yellows and blues   (d) greens and reds.

2 Find the difference between the **second round** scores of the

(a) reds and yellows   (b) greens and blues

(c) blues and reds   (d) yellows and greens.

3 Find the **third round** score for each team.

• The green team scored
  90 less than the blue team.

• The green team scored
  150 less than the red team.

• The red team scored
  120 more than the yellow team.

4 Which team's **total** score was

(a) highest   (b) lowest?

5 (a) $430 - ■ = 310$ (b) $580 - ■ = 470$ (c) $750 - ■ = 640$

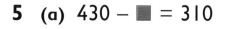

1 Choose one parcel from each shelf to make a pair with a price difference of

(a) £8   (b) £200   (c) £70   (d) £120

2 Make up two prices with a difference of £38 to put on the red parcels.

3 How much money did each person start with?

(a) 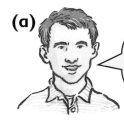 I spent £18.
I have £287 left.

(b) I spent £160.
I have £410 left.

4 How much money does each person have left?

(a)  I started with £1000.

I spent £400.

I gave away £240.

I lost half of what was left.

(b) I started with £900.

I gave away £150.

I spent £350.

I kept one quarter of what was left.

1 Use 3 of these digits each time.
Copy and complete.

0 0 2 6 3 5

(a) ▢▢▢ − 400 = 252   (b) 2▢0 − 1▢▢ = 130

2 Use these digit cards.

0 0 4 4 5 6 6 7 8 8 9

Make a pair of 3-digit numbers with a difference of

(a) 220   (b) 30   (c) 19   (d) 8.

3 Each player has two **Connection cards**.

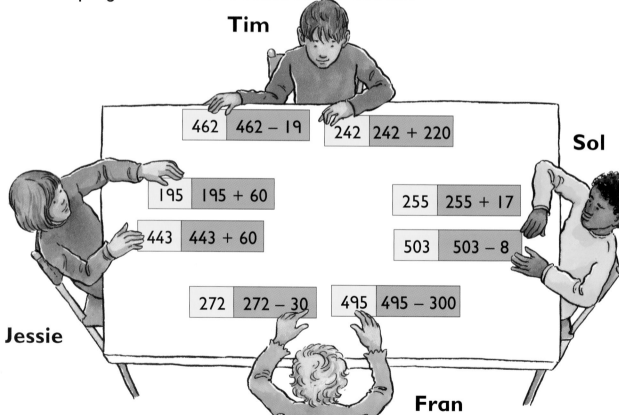

Tim

| 462 | 462 − 19 | | 242 | 242 + 220 |

Sol

| 195 | 195 + 60 |

| 443 | 443 + 60 |

| 255 | 255 + 17 |

| 503 | 503 − 8 |

| 272 | 272 − 30 | | 495 | 495 − 300 |

Jessie

Fran

Tim starts with | 462 | 462 − 19 | .

The player with the **answer** plays the next card each time.
Who is the **last** player to play?

1 June can carry 172 people. There are 31 people on board. How many more people can go on board?

	Alice	Mary	Sarah	Jane	Kate
Carries	776	663	548	384	178
Number on board	56	48	63	92	89

2 How many more people can go on board

   (a) Alice   **(b)** Mary   **(c)** Sarah   **(d)** Jane   **(e)** Kate?

3 How many more people can Alice carry than

   (a) Mary   **(b)** Sarah   **(c)** Jane   **(d)** Kate?

4 How many fewer people can Kate carry than

   (a) Jane   **(b)** Sarah   **(c)** Mary?

5 Find the difference between the number of people that can be carried by

   (a) Sarah and Mary   **(b)** Jane and Sarah

   (c) Mary and Jane.

	Air	Bally	Catto	Den	Elton	Filo
Bally	865p	–				
Catto	42p	210p	–			
Den	36p	373p	579p	–		
Elton	71p	427p	750p	645p	–	
Filo	78p	756p	988p	831p	724p	–

Write your answers in pounds and pence.

1 The notice board shows ticket prices for boat trips.
How much is the trip between

   (a) Air and Den   **(b)** Bally and Elton
   (c) Filo and Catto   **(d)** Elton and Air?

2 How much dearer is the trip from Air to Bally
than from Air to

   (a) Catto   **(b)** Den   **(c)** Elton   **(d)** Filo?

3 Find the difference in cost between trips from Bally to Filo
and from

   (a) Bally to Catto   **(b)** Bally to Den   **(c)** Bally to Elton.

4 How much cheaper is the trip from Catto to Den
than from Catto to

   (a) Elton   **(b)** Filo?

5 What is the price difference between these trips?

   (a) Den to Elton and Den to Filo

   (b) Den to Elton and Elton to Filo

   (c) Den to Filo and Elton to Filo.

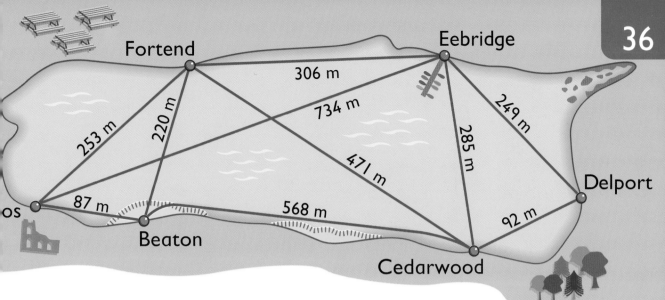

1 What is the length, in metres, of each boat trip?

(a) Cedarwood → Delport → Eebridge

(b) Aros → Beaton → Cedarwood

(c) Aros → Fortend → Eebridge

(d) Beaton → Cedarwood → Eebridge

(e) Fortend → Beaton → Aros → Fortend

(f) Delport → Eebridge → Cedarwood → Delport

2 How much longer is the trip

(a) from Beaton to Cedarwood than from Cedarwood to Delport

(b) from Aros to Fortend than from Aros to Beaton

(c) from Eebridge to Aros than from Eebridge to Fortend

(d) from Fortend to Cedarwood than from Eebridge to Cedarwood?

3 Which trip is longer and by how many metres?

(a) Cedarwood → Eebridge → Fortend **or** Cedarwood → Fortend

(b) Fortend → Beaton → Aros **or** Fortend → Aros

4 The *Jenny* departs from Aros and sails to two places. The total distance is 724 metres. Where does *Jenny*'s trip finish?

1 Use the digits 3 , 5 and 8 .
What is the difference between

(a) 583 and 385

(b) 835 and 538

(c) 358 and 853?

583
−385
198 → 18

835
−538
___

2 Add the **digits** in
each answer in question 1.
What do you notice?

3 Repeat questions 1 and 2 for other sets of three different digits.
What do you notice?

4 (a) Use the digits 2 , 6 and 9 .

Write • the largest possible number.

• the smallest possible number.

What is the difference between
these numbers?

(b) Do this again using the digits in
your answer to **4(a)**.... and again
using the digits in your new answer.

962
−269
693

963
−369
594

954
−459
___

5 Do question **4** again for other sets of three digits.
What do you notice?

I How many cakes are on

(a) 6 red plates   (b) 7 green plates   (c) 4 blue plates

(d) 3 green plates   (e) 10 blue plates   (f) 8 red plates

(g) 5 blue and 4 green plates (h) 9 green and 3 red plates?

2

 **4p**    **10p**    **7p**

Find the cost of

(a) 7    (b) 6   (c) 3   (d) 8

(e) 2  and 9    (f) 10  and 5 .

3 Zoe buys 5 and 4 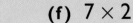 . What is her change from 50p?

4

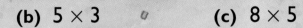

(a) 2 × 9   (b) 5 × 3   (c) 8 × 5

(d) 4 × 3   (e) 3 × 9   (f) 7 × 2

(g) 7 multiplied by 10   (h) 5 multiplied by 5

5 (a) 2 × ■ = 16   (b) 4 × ■ = 0   (c) 6 × ■ = 30

(d) ■ × 10 = 30   (e) ■ × 4 = 28   (f) ■ × 3 = 27

1 There are 10 cookies in a bag.
How many cookies are in

(a) 14 bags   (b) 70 bags

(c) 22 bags   (d) 38 bags

(e) 291 bags   (f) 103 bags?

2 Rolls are baked on trays of 100.
How many rolls are on

(a) 6 trays   (b) 10 trays

(c) 18 trays   (d) 35 trays

(e) 87 trays   (f) 70 trays?

3 Each **packet** has   Each **box** has
10 cake cases.   100 cake cases.

How many cake cases are in

(a) 19 packets   (b) 11 boxes   (c) 54 packets   (d) 66 boxes

(e) 12 boxes and 7 packets   (f) 5 boxes and 23 packets?

4 (a) $10 \times \blacksquare = 190$ (b) $\blacksquare \times 100 = 5000$

(c) $100 \times \blacksquare = 7800$ (d) $\blacksquare \times 84 = 8400$

(e) $41 \times \blacksquare = 410$ (f) $\blacksquare \times 136 = 1360$

1 Find the cost of

(a) 8 Space books   (b) 5 Dinosaur books

(c) 9 Dinosaur books   (d) 8 Joke books

(e) 8 Dinosaur books and 1 Space book.

2 Books are packed in boxes of 8.
How many books are in

(a) 4 boxes   (b) 3 boxes

(c) 10 boxes   (d) 6 boxes?

3

Each shelf holds 8 books.
How many books are on

(a) 2 shelves   (b) 5 shelves

(c) 9 shelves   (d) 7 shelves?

4 Sue bought three £8 and eight £5 tokens. How much did she pay altogether?

5 (a) $8 \times \blacksquare = 48$ (b) $8 \times \blacksquare = 8$ (c) $8 \times \blacksquare = 32$

(d) $\blacksquare \times 8 = 0$ (e) $\blacksquare \times 8 = 56$ (f) $\blacksquare \times 8 = 80$

1 How many are in

(a) 6 packs of crayons

(b) 6 packs of pencils

(c) 9 packs of pens

(d) 10 packs of pens?

2

Find the cost of

(a) 6 red bookmarks

(b) 3 blue bookmarks

(c) 6 green bookmarks

(d) 8 blue and 2 green bookmarks.

3 Felt-tip pens are sold in mini-packs of 8 and jumbo-packs of 25.

(a) Who has more pens?

(b) How many more?

I have 6 mini-packs.

Julie

I have 2 jumbo-packs.

Dave

4 (a) $6 \times \blacksquare = 36$

(b) $6 \times \blacksquare = 0$

(c) $6 \times \blacksquare = 54$

(d) $\blacksquare \times 6 = 60$

(e) $\blacksquare \times 6 = 24$

(f) $\blacksquare \times 6 = 6$

1 A shop delivers 9 copies of *Garden Magazine* each week.

How many are delivered in

(a) 3 weeks   **(b)** 7 weeks

(c) 10 weeks   **(d)** 9 weeks?

2 This week's copy has free packs of seeds.

How many seeds are in

(a) 9 packs of cucumber   **(b)** 9 packs of peas

(c) 4 packs of beans   **(d)** 8 packs of beans?

3

Garden Magazine Competition

Use the code to find the plant of the week.

(a) 9 times 9   **(b)** 5 x 9

(c) 9 x 7   **(d)** 10 nines

(e) 6 nines   **(f)** 9 times 2

54 → S		63 → D
45 → A		81 → R
72 → P		18 → H
90 → I		36 → C

4 **(a)** $9 \times \blacksquare = 36$ **(b)** $9 \times \blacksquare = 9$ **(c)** $9 \times \blacksquare = 63$

(d) $\blacksquare \times 9 = 72$ **(e)** $\blacksquare \times 9 = 27$ **(f)** $\blacksquare \times 9 = 81$

I How many are in **seven** *Funtubs*?

(a)    (b)   (c)   (d)

(e)    (f)    (g)    (h)

2 (a) 7×2 (b) 9×7 (c) 7×0 (d) 10×7

   (e) 5×7 (f) 7×1 (g) 4×7 (h) 8×7

3

Mini-tub £2 FUNTUBS — With **4** free stickers

Midi-tub £5 FUNTUBS — With **7** free stickers

Maxi-tub £7 FUNTUBS — With **10** free stickers

Find the cost of

(a) 7 *Mini-tubs*   (b) 9 *Maxi-tubs*   (c) 7 *Midi-tubs*.

4 How many *free stickers* come with

(a) 7 *Maxi-tubs*   (b) 8 *Midi-tubs*   (c) 7 *Mini-tubs*?

5 (a) $7 \times \blacksquare = 49$ (b) $7 \times \blacksquare = 42$ (c) $7 \times \blacksquare = 70$

   (d) $\blacksquare \times 7 = 21$ (e) $\blacksquare \times 7 = 0$ (f) $\blacksquare \times 7 = 14$

   (g) $7 \times \blacksquare = 63$ (h) $\blacksquare \times 7 = 7$ (i) $7 \times \blacksquare = 35$

1 Answer the questions on the cracker cards.

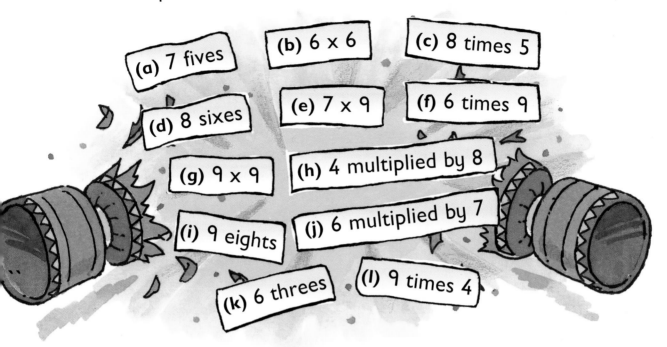

(a) 7 fives

(b) 6 × 6

(c) 8 times 5

(d) 8 sixes

(e) 7 × 9

(f) 6 times 9

(g) 9 × 9

(h) 4 multiplied by 8

(i) 9 eights

(j) 6 multiplied by 7

(k) 6 threes

(l) 9 times 4

2 How many crackers are in

(a) 6 *Prize* boxes
(b) 4 *Party* boxes
(c) 5 *Giant* boxes
(d) 7 *Party* boxes
(e) 3 *Prize* boxes
(f) 10 *Fun* boxes
(g) 9 *Party* boxes
(h) 8 *Prize* boxes
(i) 10 *Giant* boxes
(j) 5 *Fun* boxes?

6 Fun Crackers

7 Party Crackers

8 Prize Crackers

9 Giant Crackers

3

(a) 7 × 3
(b) 8 × 2
(c) 9 × 6
(d) 7 × 8
(e) 6 × 4
(f) 6 × 7
(g) 8 × 10
(h) 9 × 3
(i) 8 × 0
(j) 7 × 10
(k) 8 × 7
(l) 6 × 1

4 (a) $9 \times \blacksquare = 18$
(b) $8 \times \blacksquare = 72$
(c) $6 \times \blacksquare = 48$
(d) $\blacksquare \times 7 = 0$
(e) $\blacksquare \times 1 = 9$
(f) $\blacksquare \times 7 = 49$

1 Find the cost of each item on Mr Brown's list.

Garden Job

(a) 3 metres of fencing

(b) 4 litres of wood stain

(c) 5 tubs of concrete

(d) 20 bags of gravel

2 (a) 4 × 18   (b) 3 × 26   (c) 5 × 12   (d) 2 × 39

(e) 3 × 37   (f) 4 × 25   (g) 5 × 19   (h) 4 × 40

(i) 5 × 17   (j) 4 × 30   (k) 5 × 28   (l) 4 × 23

(m) 2 × 47   (n) 5 × 15   (o) 3 × 29   (p) 5 × 26

3

(a) 20 × 16   (b) 20 × 33   (c) 20 × 19

(d) 20 × 20   (e) 20 × 45   (f) 20 × 50

1 How many cards are in

(a) 2 Cartoon packets (b) 5 Pop packets (c) 3 Sport packets

(d) 2 Film packets (e) 5 Cartoon packets (f) 4 Film packets

(g) 4 Pop packets (h) 5 Film packets (i) 5 Sport packets?

2 (a) 3×60 (b) 4×50 (c) 5×70 (d) 4×90

(e) 2×80 (f) 3×90 (g) 4×40 (h) 5×50

(i) $2 \times \blacksquare = 100$ (j) $3 \times \blacksquare = 210$ (k) $4 \times \blacksquare = 320$

3 Find the **approximate** cost of

(a) 5 CDs (b) 4 Games (c) 3 Keyboards

(d) 2 Games (e) 5 Keyboards (f) 3 Paintboxes.

4

Ben

I have £149.

Estimate.
Does Ben have enough money
to buy 5 Video Sets?
Explain.

1 Copy and complete. Try to find **two** answers each time.

(a) ■ × ▲ = 42   (b) ■ × ▲ = 63   (c) ■ × ▲ = 72

(d) ■ × ▲ = 54   (e) ■ × ▲ = 56   (f) ■ × ▲ = 48

2 Write a **pair** of numbers which have

(a) a sum of 11 and a product of 24

(b) a sum of 13 and a product of 36

(c) a sum of 14 and a product of 49

(d) a difference of 3 and a product of 70

(e) a difference of 0 and a product of 64.

3 Find **different** ways of completing each multiplication.

(a) ■ ▲ × ◆ = 80   (b) ■ ▲ × ◆ = 120

4 Find each child's **starting** number.

(a) I add 5 and multiply by 10. My answer is 630.

(b) I subtract 2 and multiply by 100. My answer is 3400.

(c) I add 4 and multiply by 3. My answer is 90.

(d) I take away 3 and multiply by 4. My answer is 88.

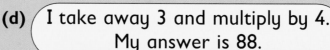

1 What is the weight of

(a) 2 crates of oranges

(b) 3 crates of bananas

(c) 4 crates of melons

(d) 5 crates of pears?

2 Which weighs more

(a) 5 crates of melons or 3 crates of oranges

(b) 3 crates of pears or 2 crates of melons

(c) 3 crates of melons or 2 crates of bananas?

3 Find the cost of each order.

ORDER NAME	ITEM	NUMBER OF SACKS
Smith	Coffee	2
Younis	Sugar	4
Bloggs	Salt	3
Amin	Flour	5

4 Which costs less

(a) 5 sacks of salt or 4 sacks of flour

(b) 5 sacks of sugar or 4 sacks of coffee?

1 How many tents?

(a) 14 cubs – 2 in each tent (b) 20 cubs – 4 in each tent

(c) 45 cubs – 5 in each tent (d) 12 cubs – 3 in each tent

(e) 60 cubs – 10 in each tent (f) 30 cubs – 3 in each tent

2 Divide equally among the tents.

(a) 5 cubs in 5 tents (b) 28 cubs in 4 tents

(c) 24 cubs in 3 tents (d) 30 cubs in 10 tents

(e) 8 cubs in 4 tents (f) 25 cubs in 5 tents

3 (a) 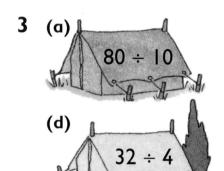 $80 \div 10$ (b) $20 \div 5$ (c) $27 \div 3$

(d) 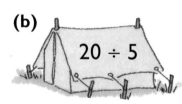 $32 \div 4$ (e) $0 \div 2$ (f) 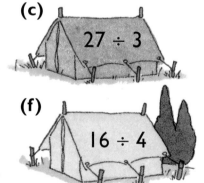 $16 \div 4$

4 (a) $\blacksquare \div 3 = 6$ (b) $\blacksquare \div 2 = 9$ (c) $\blacksquare \div 5 = 4$

(d) $40 \div \blacksquare = 10$ (e) $70 \div \blacksquare = 7$ (f) $15 \div \blacksquare = 5$

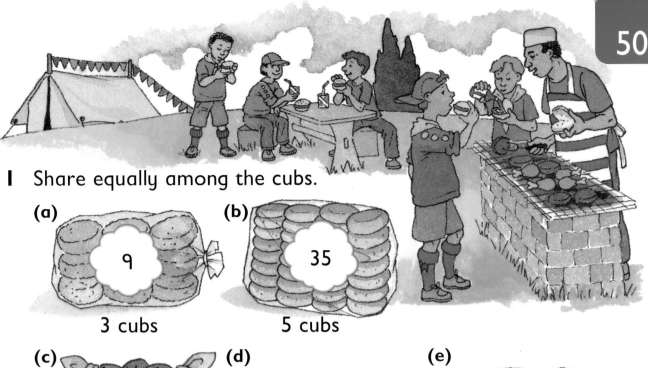

1 Share equally among the cubs.

(a) 9 — 3 cubs

(b) 35 — 5 cubs

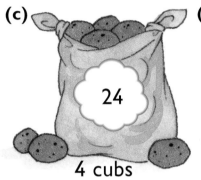

(c) 24 — 4 cubs

(d) 21 — 3 cubs

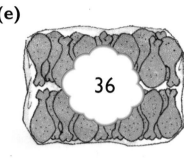

(e) 36 — 4 cubs

2 **(a)** Divide 100 by 10. **(b)** How many groups of 5 in 15?

   (c) Zero divided by 4 **(d)** Share 12 equally among 3.

   (e) Half of 16 **(f)** How many fives make 30?

   (g) Divide 40 by 10. **(h)** One quarter of 4

3 **(a)** $\blacksquare \div 3 = 2$ **(b)** $\blacksquare \div 10 = 9$ **(c)** $\blacksquare \div 2 = 5$

   (d) $50 \div \blacksquare = 10$ **(e)** $32 \div \blacksquare = 8$ **(f)** $27 \div \blacksquare = 9$

4 There are **between** 20 and 50 flags. They can be shared equally among 2 tents **or** 4 tents **or** 5 tents.

How many flags are there?

1 Eight children can sit in each log.
How many logs are needed for
  (a) 40 children   **(b)** 56 children
  (c) 16 children   **(d)** 48 children
  (e) 24 children   **(f)** 72 children?

2 **(a)** Divide 64 by 8.   **(b)** How many eights make 56?
  (c) 16 divided by 8   **(d)** Divide 32 equally among 8.
  (e) Divide 80 by 8.   **(f)** 8 shared equally among 8.
  (g) 48 divided by 8   **(h)** Group 24 in eights.

3 **(a)** $72 \div 8 = \blacksquare$ **(b)** $8 \div 8 = \blacksquare$ **(c)** $0 \div 8 = \blacksquare$
  (d) $\blacksquare \div 8 = 8$ **(e)** $\blacksquare \div 8 = 4$ **(f)** $\blacksquare \div 8 = 10$

2 **(a)** Jem spent £40 on T-shirts. How many did she buy?

  (b) Sara spent £64 on books and towels. She bought **three times as many** books as towels. How many of each did she buy?

1 Each ride takes six children at a time.

How many rides are needed for

(a) 18 children (b) 42 children (c) 60 children

(d) 30 children (e) 54 children (f) 12 children?

2 (a) 6 divided by 6 (b) How many sixes make 36?

(c) Divide 24 by 6. (d) Share 12 equally among 6.

(e) Divide 36 by 6. (f) How many groups of 6 are in 48?

(g) 0 divided by 6 (h) Divide 60 equally among 6.

3  How many videos can you buy for

(a) £30 (b) £54 (c) £42?

4 (a) $48 \div 6 = \blacksquare$ (b) $6 \div 6 = \blacksquare$ (c) $24 \div 6 = \blacksquare$

(d) $\blacksquare \div 6 = 3$ (e) $\blacksquare \div 6 = 10$ (f) $\blacksquare \div 6 = 0$

53

I Each player needs 9 Snap cards.
How many children can play?

(a) 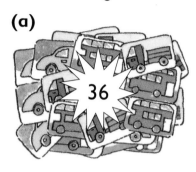 36

(b) 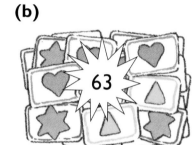 63

(c) 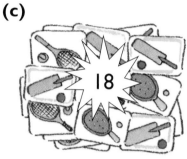 18

(d) 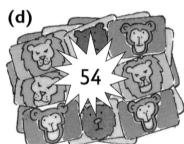 54

(e)  72

(f) 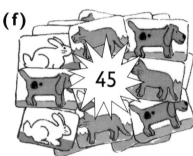 45

2 **(a)** 81 divided by 9   **(b)** 9 shared equally among 9

   (c) Divide 27 by 9.   **(d)** How many groups of are 9 in 90?

   (e) Divide 0 by 9.   **(f)** How many nines make 45?

   (g) 36 divided by 9   **(h)** Divide 72 equally among 9.

3 How many dice can you buy
when you spend

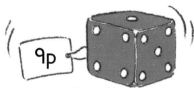

   (a) 18p   **(b)** 63p   **(c)** 54p   **(d)** 81p?

4 **(a)** $9 \div 9 = \blacksquare$ **(b)** $90 \div 9 = \blacksquare$ **(c)** $27 \div 9 = \blacksquare$

   (d) $\blacksquare \div 9 = 5$ **(e)** $\blacksquare \div 9 = 8$ **(f)** $\blacksquare \div 9 = 0$

1 The cart carries 7 children on each trip.
How many trips are needed for

(a) 21 children   (b) 56 children

(c) 35 children   (d) 70 children

(e) 42 children   (f) 63 children?

2 (a) Divide 28 by 7.   (b) Share 49 equally among 7.

(c) 7 divided by 7   (d) How many sevens make 14?

(e) Divide 35 by 7.   (f) How many groups of 7 are in 63?

(g) 0 divided by 7   (h) Divide 21 equally among 7.

3 (a) $42 \div 7 = \blacksquare$ (b) $56 \div 7 = \blacksquare$ (c) $0 \div 7 = \blacksquare$

(d) $\blacksquare \div 7 = 4$ (e) $\blacksquare \div 7 = 7$ (f) $\blacksquare \div 7 = 1$

4 Tickets for the cart ride cost 7p each.
How many tickets can you buy
when you spend

(a) 14p   (b) 70p   (c) 35p

(d) 63p   (e) 21p   (f) 56p?

5 Mel bought **twice as many** tickets
as Adam for the cart ride.
Together their tickets cost 63p.
How many tickets did each buy?

1 Share equally among the trays.

    (a) 60 sardines ⟶ 6 trays   (b) 21 trout ⟶ 7 trays

    (c) 54 cod ⟶ 9 trays   (d) 70 herring ⟶ 7 trays

    (e) 12 haddock ⟶ 6 trays   (f) 45 salmon ⟶ 9 trays

    (g) 49 plaice ⟶ 7 trays   (h) 72 sole ⟶ 9 trays

2 (a) Divide 9 by 9.   (b) 48 divided equally among 6

    (c) 28 divided by 7   (d) How many fives make 45?

    (e) Divide 0 by 8.   (f) How many groups of 6 are in 18?

    (g) 63 divided by 7   (h) Share 16 equally between 2.

3 (a) $63 \div 9 = \blacksquare$ (b) $6 \div 6 = \blacksquare$ (c) $0 \div 7 = \blacksquare$

    (d) $\blacksquare \div 6 = 9$ (e) $\blacksquare \div 7 = 8$ (f) $\blacksquare \div 9 = 0$

    (g) $30 \div \blacksquare = 5$ (h) $32 \div \blacksquare = 8$ (i) $81 \div \blacksquare = 9$

4 How many sardines can you buy?

    (a) Spend 40p.   (b) Spend 80p.

    (c) Spend 32p.   (d) Spend 48p.

8p each

5 Mark bought **half as many** sardines as Emma.
Together their sardines cost 72p.
How many sardines did each buy?

1 Copy and complete.

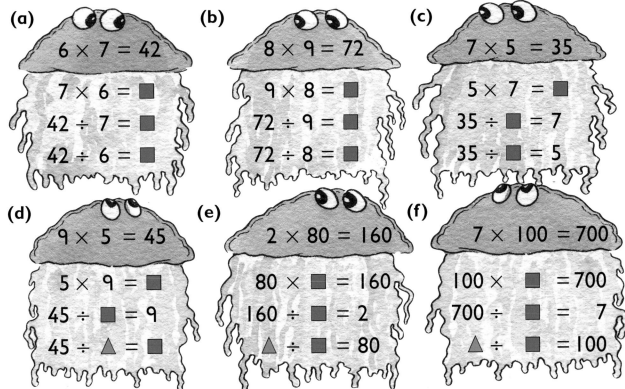

(a)
6 × 7 = 42
7 × 6 = ■
42 ÷ 7 = ■
42 ÷ 6 = ■

(b)
8 × 9 = 72
9 × 8 = ■
72 ÷ 9 = ■
72 ÷ 8 = ■

(c)
7 × 5 = 35
5 × 7 = ■
35 ÷ ■ = 7
35 ÷ ■ = 5

(d)
9 × 5 = 45
5 × 9 = ■
45 ÷ ■ = 9
45 ÷ ▲ = ■

(e)
2 × 80 = 160
80 × ■ = 160
160 ÷ ■ = 2
▲ ÷ ■ = 80

(f)
7 × 100 = 700
100 × ■ = 700
700 ÷ ■ = 7
▲ ÷ ■ = 100

2 Use the multiplication fact. Write two division stories.

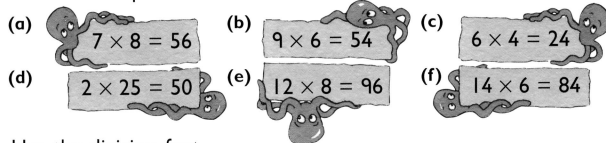

(a) 7 × 8 = 56
(b) 9 × 6 = 54
(c) 6 × 4 = 24
(d) 2 × 25 = 50
(e) 12 × 8 = 96
(f) 14 × 6 = 84

3 Use the division fact.

Write two multiplication stories and a **different** division story.

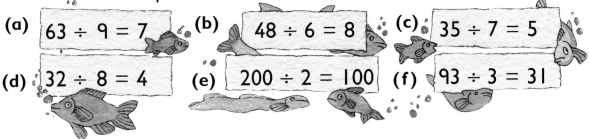

(a) 63 ÷ 9 = 7
(b) 48 ÷ 6 = 8
(c) 35 ÷ 7 = 5
(d) 32 ÷ 8 = 4
(e) 200 ÷ 2 = 100
(f) 93 ÷ 3 = 31

4 Write four number stories each time.

(a) 2 34 68   (b) 10 7 70   (c) 9 100 900

1 Copy and complete.

(a)

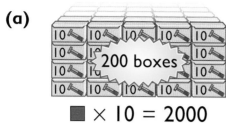

$$\blacksquare \times 10 = 2000$$
$$2000 \div 10 = \blacksquare$$

(b)

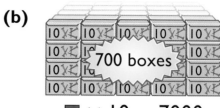

$$\blacksquare \times 10 = 7000$$
$$7000 \div 10 = \blacksquare$$

(c)

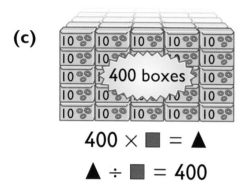

$$400 \times \blacksquare = \blacktriangle$$
$$\blacktriangle \div \blacksquare = 400$$

(d)

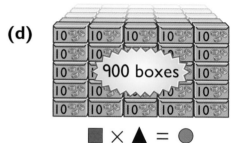

$$\blacksquare \times \blacktriangle = \bullet$$
$$\bullet \div \blacktriangle = \blacksquare$$

2 **(a)** $5000 \div 10 = \blacksquare$ **(b)** $8000 \div 10 = \blacksquare$ **(c)** $6000 \div 10 = \blacksquare$

(d) $\blacksquare \div 10 = 300$ **(e)** $\blacksquare \div 10 = 100$ **(f)** $\blacksquare \div 10 = 1000$

3 Copy and complete.

(a)

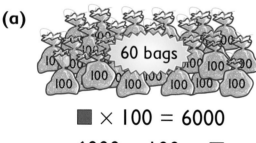

$$\blacksquare \times 100 = 6000$$
$$6000 \div 100 = \blacksquare$$

(b)

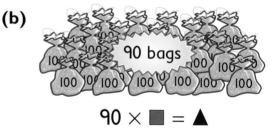

$$90 \times \blacksquare = \blacktriangle$$
$$\blacktriangle \div \blacksquare = 90$$

4 **(a)** $3000 \div 100 = \blacksquare$ **(b)** $8000 \div 100 = \blacksquare$ **(c)** $7000 \div 100 = \blacksquare$

(d) $\blacksquare \div 100 = 50$ **(e)** $\blacksquare \div 100 = 10$ **(f)** $\blacksquare \div 100 = 40$

5 What happens to the digits of these numbers when you

(a) divide by 100 **(b)** divide by 10?

1 Share the cards equally between two shelves.

(a) 24   (b) 36   (c) 28

2 Share the cards equally among three shelves.

(a) 39   (b) 57   (c) 48

3 How many **4p** cards can you buy for

   (a) 44p   (b) 68p

   (c) 56p   (d) 76p?

4 How many **5p** cards can you buy for

   (a) 75p   (b) 90p

   (c) 65p   (d) 80p?

5 (a) Divide 66 by 6.   (b) How many sevens make 84?

   (c) 90 divided by 6   (d) Share 96 equally among 8.

   (e) 91 divided by 7   (f) How many groups of six are in 84?

   (g) Divide 88 by 8.   (h) Divide 98 equally among 7.

1 These cards are shared equally among three shelves.
How many cards go on each shelf and how many are left over?

(a)
44

(b) **37**

(c)
56

2 These cards are shared equally among four shelves.
How many cards go on each shelf and how many are left over?

(a) 50 cards   (b) 75 cards   (c) 65 cards

3 How many boxes can be filled with cards?
How many cards are left over?

	(a)	(b)	(c)	(d)	(e)
Number of cards	27	74	71	93	81
Number in each box	2	6	5	8	7

4 How many cards can you buy?
How much money do you have left?

	(a)	(b)	(c)	(d)	(e)	(f)
You have...	83p	35p	94p	89p	99p	£1
Each card costs...	6p	2p	7p	5p	8p	9p

5 Find the missing numbers.

(a) $32 = (6 \times 5) + \blacksquare$ (b) $45 = (7 \times 6) + \blacksquare$

(c) $39 = (4 \times 9) + \blacksquare$ (d) $39 = (5 \times 7) + \blacksquare$

(e) $85 = (10 \times 8) + \blacksquare$ (f) $438 = (100 \times 4) + \blacksquare$

(g) $(18 \div \blacksquare) + 2 = 8$ (h) $(54 \div \blacksquare) - 3 = 6$

(i) $(\blacksquare \div 8) + 4 = 9$

1 How many taxis are needed to take 29 children on the school trip when each taxi takes

    (a) 2 children   **(b)** 4 children

    (c) 3 children   **(d)** 5 children?

2 How many games teams can be made?

	Class 2	Class 3	Class 4	Class 5	Class 6
Number of children	26	23	34	26	36
Number in each team	3	4	10	4	5

3 How many picnic groups can be formed?
How many extra children are there?

	(a)	(b)	(c)	(d)	(e)	(f)
Number of children	49	58	63	52	65	38
Number in each group	6	8	7	9	10	8

4 The taxi with 4 children costs £15.
What is the cost for each child?

5 Find the cost for each child travelling in these minibuses.

(a)

Takes 5 for £11.

(b)

Takes 10 for £17.

1 How much money does each child have?

2 Write in order, starting with the **largest** amount.

(a) £7·03, £6·85, £7·00, £6·98   (b) £10·30, £11·26, £9·72, £10·0[

(c) £14·08, £15·18, £14·66, £14·80   (d) £19·70, £20·05, £19·07, £20·(

3 List the notes and coins for the amounts spent.

4 Choose from these notes and coins. List five different ways of making £20.

How much money does each child have, **to the nearest pound**?

Round each amount **to the nearest pound**.

(a) £6·98 (b) £3·72 (c) £12·24 (d) £16·80

(e) £19·09 (f) £23·45 (g) £34·55 (h) £45·61

Mousetrap! £11·30

4 in-a-row £4·79

Battleships £7·15

Beat-the-Clock £5·95

Round the prices to the nearest pound and **estimate** the total cost of

(a) Mousetrap and Battleships (b) Battleships and 4 in-a-row

(c) Mousetrap, 4 in-a-row and Battleships

(d) Mousetrap, Battleships and Beat-the-Clock.

Explain your answer each time.

Use the prices rounded to the nearest pound. **Estimate** if you can buy

(a) Beat-the-Clock and 4 in-a-row with a £10 note

(b) Battleships, 4 in-a-row and Beat-the-Clock with a £20 note.

70p

£1·20

£3·50

£1·10

£1·40

80p

90p

£2·60

£1·70

1 Find the total cost of.

(a) , and   (b) , and

(c)  , and   (d) , and

(e)  , ,  and

(f) 3   (g) 4   (h) 3   (i) 4

2 Zoë buys 3 different items.
She spends £2·90.
What could she buy?

3 Sami buys 4 items altogether.
He spends between £9 and £10.
What could he buy?

4 (a) £1·70 + ■ = £2·40   (b) £1·10 + ■ = £2·30

(c) £2·60 + ■ = £3·50   (d) £3·50 + ■ = £5·00

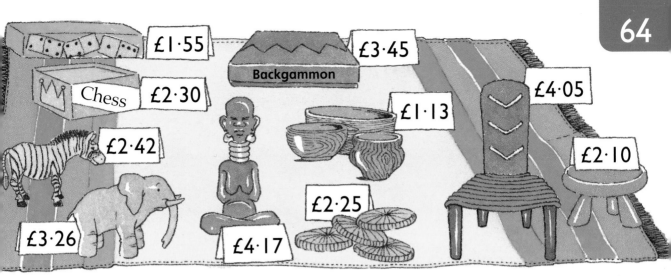

1 Find the total cost of

(a)  and 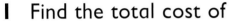   (b)  and

(c)  and   (d) and

(e) Backgammon and   (f) and Backgammon

(g) and Chess and Backgammon   (h) and and

2 Suzi spent £3·65 altogether.
She bought 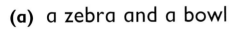 and one other item.

What was the other item she bought?

3 Find the total cost of
(a) a zebra and a bowl   (b) a statue and an elephant
(c) a bowl and an elephant   (d) a zebra and a statue
(e) an elephant and a zebra   (f) a statue and a bowl.

4 Anja bought 2 bowls, a statue and an elephant.
How much did she spend altogether?

Money: totals, multiples of 5p, 1p

1 List the coins in each person's change.

(a)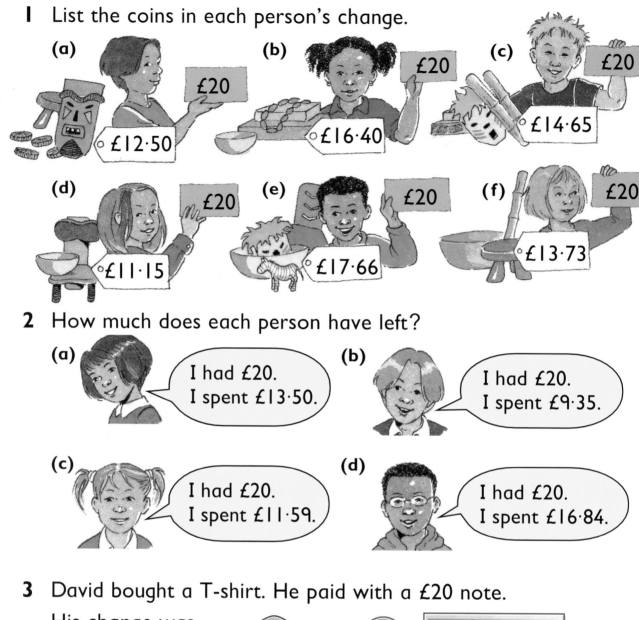
£20
£12·50

(b)
£20
£16·40

(c)
£20
£14·65

(d)
£20
£11·15

(e)
£20
£17·66

(f)
£20
£13·73

2 How much does each person have left?

(a) I had £20. I spent £13·50.

(b) I had £20. I spent £9·35.

(c) I had £20. I spent £11·59.

(d) I had £20. I spent £16·84.

3 David bought a T-shirt. He paid with a £20 note.

His change was

How much did he spend?

4 Alana bought a book. She paid with a £20 note.
Her change was

How much did she spend?

African Wildlife Exhibition

Entrance

Adults   £4·50
Children   £2·60

Jack   Ben   Mia   Jay
      Fran

1 How much did it cost for the group to visit the exhibition?

2 Jack bought 3 animal pictures.

£4·25 each

   (a) How much did they cost altogether?

   (b) What was Jack's change from £20?

3 Jay had saved eight 50p coins and six 20p coins for the visit. How much had he saved altogether?

4 Mia spent one half of her savings on a book. The book cost £4·75. How much had she saved?

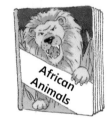

5 Ben spent one quarter of his savings on a video. He had saved £16·40. How much did the video cost?

Africa

6 Fran spent £2·54 on drinks, £3·12 on food and £4·38 on gifts. Will she be able to pay using a £10 note? Explain your answer.

African Wildlife Exhibition

1 How many shapes in each set are coloured?

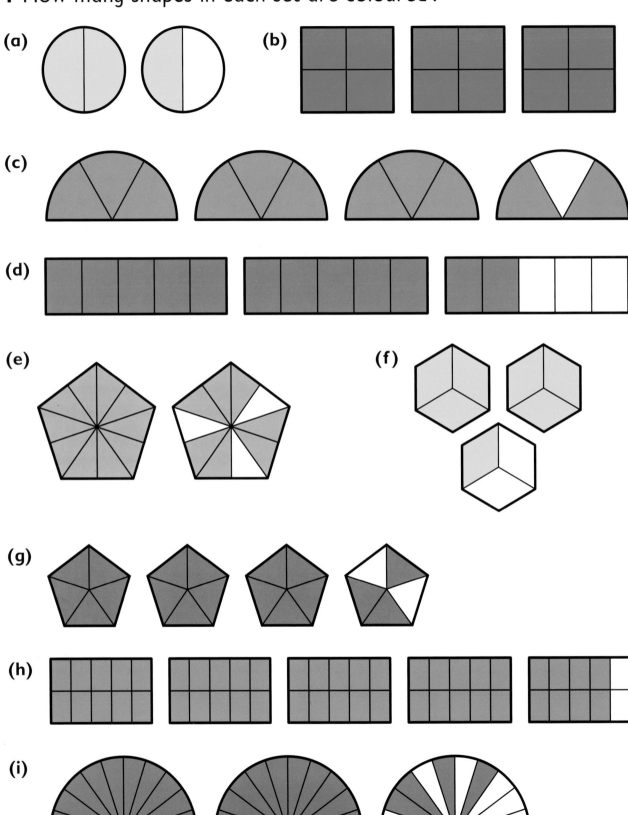

(a)

(b)

(c)

(d)

(e)

(f)

(g)

(h)

(i)

1 Find

(a) $\frac{1}{2}$ of 14

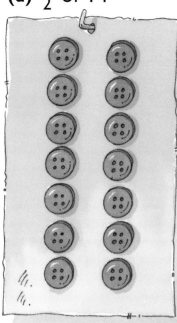

(b) $\frac{1}{4}$ of 16

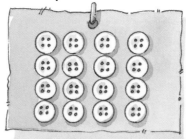

(c) $\frac{1}{10}$ of 30

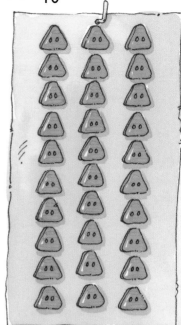

(d) $\frac{1}{3}$ of 9

(e) $\frac{1}{5}$ of 20.

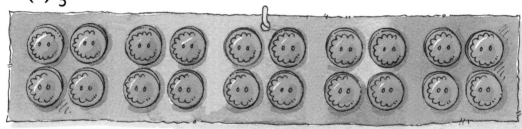

2

(a) $\frac{1}{5}$ of 40

(b) $\frac{1}{10}$ of 50

(c) one third of 18

(d) $\frac{1}{4}$ of 28

(e) $\frac{1}{2}$ of 20

(f) one tenth of 100

(g) $\frac{1}{3}$ of 27

(h) $\frac{1}{10}$ of 80

(i) one fifth of 45

(j) $\frac{1}{3}$ of 15

(k) $\frac{1}{5}$ of 50

(l) one third of 21

3 Kim had 30 buttons. She gave $\frac{1}{5}$ of them to Jon and $\frac{1}{3}$ of the rest to Rona.

How many buttons have
(a) Jon   **(b)** Rona   **(c)** Kim?

1 Copy and complete each equal fractions story.

(a)

$$\frac{\blacksquare}{2} = \frac{\blacksquare}{10}$$

(b)

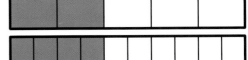

$$\frac{2}{\blacksquare} = \frac{\blacksquare}{10}$$

(c)

$$\frac{1}{\blacksquare} = \frac{\blacksquare}{6}$$

(d)

$$\frac{\blacksquare}{4} = \frac{6}{\blacksquare}$$

(e)

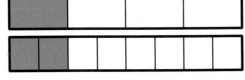

$$\frac{\blacksquare}{5} = \frac{8}{\blacksquare}$$

(f)

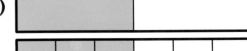

$$\frac{1}{\blacksquare} = \frac{3}{\blacksquare}$$

(g)

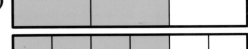

$$\frac{\blacksquare}{\blacksquare} = \frac{\blacksquare}{\blacksquare}$$

(h)

$$\frac{\blacksquare}{\blacksquare} = \frac{\blacksquare}{\blacksquare}$$

(i)

$$\frac{\blacksquare}{\blacksquare} = \frac{\blacksquare}{\blacksquare} = \frac{\blacksquare}{\blacksquare}$$

1 Each child has 10 shapes to make a design.

Write in tenths **and** as a decimal the fraction of each design which is   **(a)** red   **(b)** yellow.

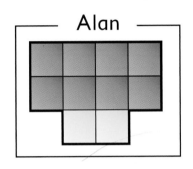

Alan

Becky

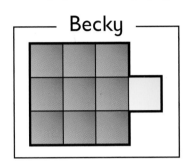

Claire

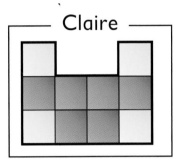

Daniel

Emma

Fergus

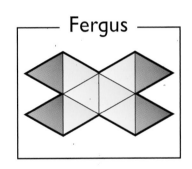

2 Write in tenths **and** as a decimal the position shown by each arrow.

(a)

(b)
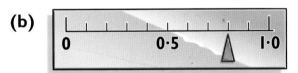

(c)
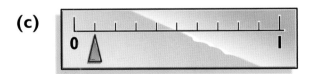

(d)
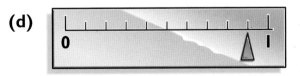

3 Write in decimal form.

(a) 7 tenths   **(b)** $\frac{1}{10}$ **(c)** 5 tenths   **(d)** $\frac{2}{10}$

1   Each **complete** tower has 10 cubes.
    Jason has made $3\frac{6}{10}$ or 3·6 towers.
    Write in fraction form **and** in decimal
    form how many towers each child has made.

2   Write in fraction form **and** in decimal form
    the position shown by each arrow.

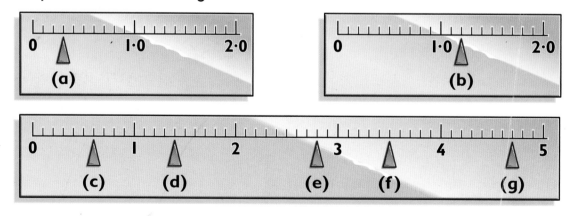

3   Write in decimal form.

    (a) $\frac{9}{10}$ (b) five and two tenths   (c) $6\frac{1}{10}$ (d) three

1 Copy and complete each decimal number sequence.

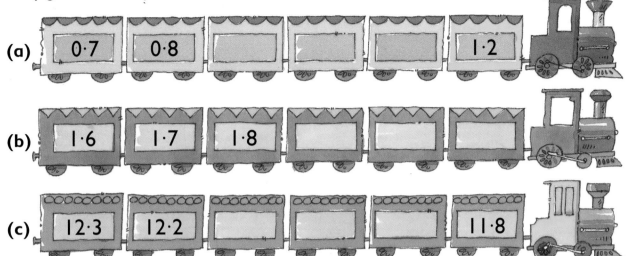

(a) | 0·7 | 0·8 | | | 1·2 |

(b) | 1·6 | 1·7 | 1·8 | | | |

(c) | 12·3 | 12·2 | | | 11·8 |

2 Write in order, starting with the **smallest** number.

(a) 1·9   2·1   1·4   (b) 4·5   5·4   5·1

(c) 3·7   3·4   4·3   3·0   4·0

3 What is the value of the digit in each green box?

(a) 13·**6**   (b) 2**1**·3   (c) **3**6·2   (d) 62·**0**

4 Write as a decimal fraction the number of tenths between each pair of red numbers.

(a) 0 0·1 0·2 0·3 0·4 0·5 0·6 0·7 0·8   (b) 0 0·1 0·2 0·3 0·4 0·5 0·6 0·7 0·8 0·9

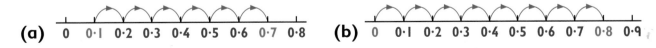

(c) 0·8 0·9 1·0 1·1 1·2 1·3 1·4   (d) 1·7 1·8 1·9 2·0 2·1 2·2 2·3 2·4

1 Write in decimal form how far each child jumped.

Alan

0 m   1 m   2 m   3 m

Becky

0 m   1 m   2 m   3 m

Claire

0 m   1 m   2 m   3 m

2 How far did each of these children jump?

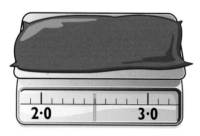

Daniel: I jumped zero point four metres further than Beth.

Emma: Alan jumped one point five metres further than I did.

3 Write as a decimal fraction the weight of each bag of sand.

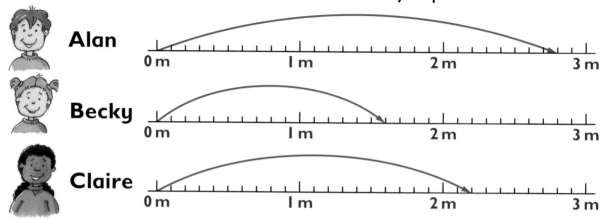

2·0   3·0   3·0   4·0   4·0   5·0

4 How heavy is each child's bag of sand?

Fergus: My sand is zero point eight kilograms lighter than the sand in the green bag.

Jason: The weight of my sand is halfway between the sand in the red and blue bags.

TOPIC ASSESSMENT

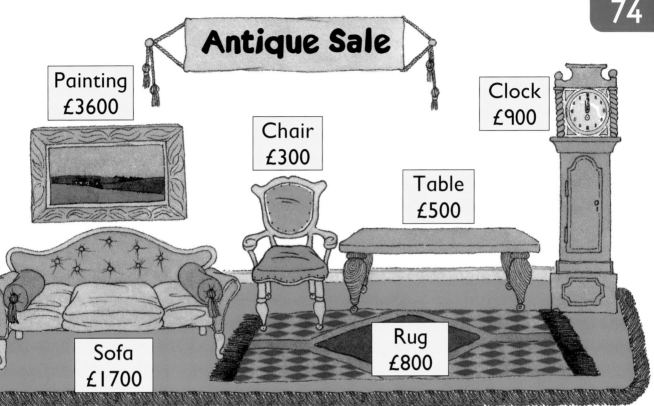

1 How much altogether would it cost to buy the

(a) Clock and Rug   (b) Chair and Clock

(c) Sofa and Chair   (d) Table and Painting

(e) Clock and Sofa   (f) Painting and Rug

(g) Clock and Painting   (h) Sofa and Rug

(i) Chair, Table and Rug?

2 (a)   800 + 300   (b) 400 + 600   (c)   700 + 700

(d) 7500 + 700   (e) 500 + 2900   (f) 4800 + 800

(g) 400 + 900 + 200   (h) 300 + 1200 + 400

3 (a)   900 + ■ = 1800   (b) ■ + 800 = 1300

(c) 5600 + ■ = 6200   (d) ■ + 7700 = 8100

1 Find each ticket number.

Anna

My number is the sum of 2700 and 900.

Rory

To make my number you double 900 and then add 500.

Su

My number is double Anna's number.

Ben

My number is the total of 30 and 2158.

David

My number is 300 more than Ben's.

Ravi

My number is double the sum of 500, 400 and 800.

Jane

My number is 43 more than Rory's.

Marie

When you add 600 to my number, you get 3000.

2 Whose ticket numbers have a difference of **(a)** 100 **(b)** 200?

3 The **winning** ticket number

- has the same tens and units digit
- is between two thousand and three thousand
- has a hundreds digit which is double its thousands digit
- has no zero.

Who has the winning ticket?

1 How many fruits are left?

(a)

1400

Eat 6.

(b)

1600

Eat 8.

(c)

1300

Eat 5.

(d)
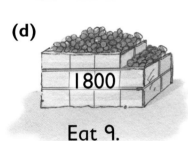
1800

Eat 9.

(e)
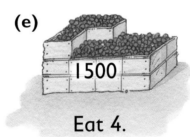
1500

Eat 4.

(f)
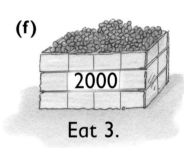
2000

Eat 3.

2 (a) 5 less than 1482
(b) Subtract 8 from 1364.
(c) 2575 minus 7
(d) Take 3 from 5211.
(e) 3147 take away 9
(f) 6 less than 7293
(g) Subtract 4 from 1402.
(h) Take 8 from 4706.
(i) 1003 subtract 5
(j) 2006 minus 7

3 (a) $2164 - \blacksquare = 2159$
(b) $2282 - \blacksquare = 2279$
(c) $\blacksquare - 6 = 4245$
(d) $\blacksquare - 8 = 1548$
(e) $3358 - \blacksquare = 3349$
(f) $4673 - \blacksquare = 4669$
(g) $\blacksquare - 7 = 6315$
(h) $\blacksquare - 9 = 1234$

Franka's Fruit Factory

Raspberry Jam — 4000
Plum Jam — 3992
Apple Juice — 2000
Orange Juice — 1996
Strawberries — 3000
Peaches — 2994

1 Find the difference between the number of

(a) jars of raspberry jam and plum jam

(b) cartons of apple juice and orange juice

(c) tins of strawberries and peaches.

2 (a) $2364 - 2358$ (b) $6541 - 6535$ (c) $3793 - 3784$

(d) $8132 - 8127$ (e) $4305 - 4299$ (f) $7803 - 7796$

3 Find the difference between the number of cartons.

(a)

1998 2006

(b)
2997 3003

(c)
2003 1994

(d)
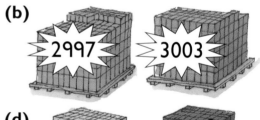
3002 2998

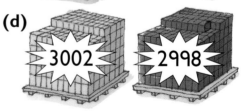

4 Find the difference between

(a) 5243 and 5229 (b) 9458 and 9474 (c) 2602 and 2587

(d) 6885 and 6901 (e) 4007 and 3994 (f) 4989 and 5005.

5 (a) $4702 - \blacksquare = 4685$ (b) $1007 - \blacksquare = 995$ (c) $2006 - \blacksquare = 1998$

(d) $\blacksquare - 15 = 2586$ (e) $\blacksquare - 14 = 1997$ (f) $\blacksquare - 19 = 3987$

Ask your teacher how to play this game for two players.

1500	1300	1100	1600	1200	1400
700	900	500	600	400	800
1400	1300	1520	1653	1721	1200
7	5	8	9	6	4
1995	1990	1999	1987	1989	1997
2006	2002	2010	2008	2004	2011

1 Janey found 3 boxes of old coins.

(a) How many coins did she find altogether?

(b) She gave Sam half of the silver coins and one quarter of the gold coins. How many coins does she have left?

(c) How many more coins would Janey need to make a total of 4000 coins?

2 Use + **or** – each time.

Copy and complete.

(a)

1900 ● 600 = 2500
2009 ● 1992 = 17
3000 ● 8 = 2992

(b)

2175 ● 18 = 2193
3265 ● 8 = 3257
1359 ● 600 = 759

3 Find the number at the bottom of each chain.

(a) 1200 → Add 400. → Subtract 9. → Add 30. → Subtract 18. → ☐

(b) 2300 → Subtract 600. → Add 85. → Subtract 7. → Add 22. → ☐

(c) 2800 → Add 500. → Subtract 7. → Subtract 93. → Find half. → ☐

I Which planes have numbers that are multiples of

(a) 2   (b) 5   (c) 10   (d) 2, 5 and 10?

16   70   95   120   35

2

Tombola Stall

• multiples of 3 win a video
• multiples of 5 win a balloon
• multiples of 3 **and** 4 win a book.

What does each of these tickets win?

27   19   55   24   32

3

Hit 3 multiples of four to win a teddy **or** 3 multiples of five to win a coconut.

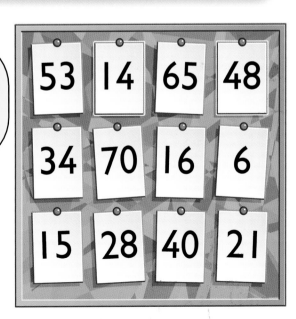

53	14	65	48
34	70	16	6
15	28	40	21

Which cards could you hit to win

(a) a teddy   (b) a coconut?

10 m
sea level 0 m
⁻10 m
⁻20 m — diver
⁻30 m
⁻40 m — shark
⁻50 m — stingray
⁻60 m — whale
⁻70 m
⁻80 m — wreck

seagull
seal
mini-sub
diving bell

The seagull is 10 metres **above** sea level.
The   seal   is 10 metres **below** sea level.

1 The seal is at a depth of ⁻10 m.
   Write the depth of each of the other things.

2 Write the position shown by each arrow on the diving bell's display

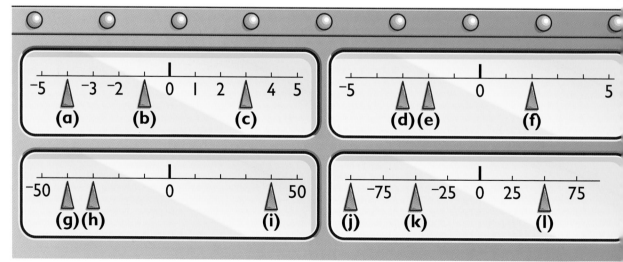

Number properties: negative numbers

The temperature is 30 °C.

The temperature is ⁻17°C.

1 Write each of these temperatures.

(a)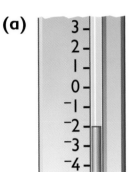

(b)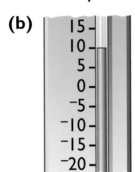

(c)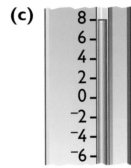

(d)

2 Which temperatures are **(a)** above freezing **(b)** below freezing?

3 Which temperature is lower? **(a)** 15°C or 19°C **(b)** ⁻7°C or 5°C

4 Which temperature is higher? **(a)** ⁻4°C or 0°C **(b)** ⁻9°C or ⁻8°C

5 Write these cities in order of temperature, **warmest** first.

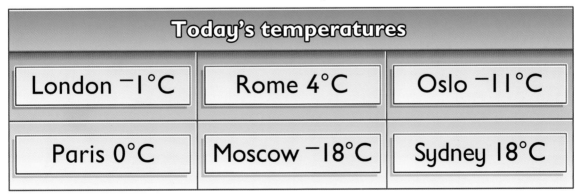

Today's temperatures		
London ⁻1°C	Rome 4°C	Oslo ⁻11°C
Paris 0°C	Moscow ⁻18°C	Sydney 18°C

6 Write three temperatures between 2 °C and ⁻3 °C.

June						
Sun	Mon	Tue	Wed	Thu	Fri	Sat
		1	2	3	4	5
6	7	8	9	10	11	12
13	14	15	16	17	18	19
20	21	22	23	24	25	26
27	28	29	30			

July						
Sun	Mon	Tue	Wed	Thu	Fri	Sat
				1	2	3
4	5	6	7	8	9	10
11	12	13	14	15	16	17
18	19	20	21	22	23	24
25	26	27	28	29	30	31

August						
Sun	Mon	Tue	Wed	Thu	Fri	Sat
1	2	3	4	5	6	7
8	9	10	11	12	13	14
15	16	17	18	19	20	21
22	23	24	25	26	27	28
29	30	31				

Mollie keeps a Summer diary.

1 Write the **day** of the week for each of these dates when she went pony-riding.

    (a) 5th June   (b) 20th June

    (c) 2nd July   (d) 22nd July

    (e) 9th August   (f) 1st September

2 Write the **date** for each of these events in Mollie's diary.

    (a) Went swimming   – second Tuesday in June

    (b) Visited Gran   – third Wednesday in July

    (c) My birthday   – first Thursday in August

    (d) Visited the zoo – last Saturday in August

Use a calendar for this year.

3 Write the **day** of the week for each of these dates.

    (a) 15th April   (b) 31st May

    (c) 23rd September   (d) 6th October

4 Write the **date** for each of these days.

    (a) First Sunday in November   (b) Third Monday in January

1 Mollie's seaside holiday was from 3rd July until 17th July.
For how many **weeks** was she on holiday?

2 For how many weeks were Mollie's friends on holiday?

	Andy	Beth	Claire	Dave	Erica
From...	18th June	9th August	24th June	21st July	26th June
Until...	25th June	30th August	29th July	18th August	7th August

3 Mollie stayed at her Gran's from 25th August until 30th August.
For how many **days** did she stay?

4 For how many days did each of these events last?

(a) Circus:
9th-12th June

(b) Regatta:
27th June-3rd July

(c) Cub camp:
30th July-8th August

(d) Fair:
26th June-28th August

Use a calendar for this year.

5 How many **weeks** are there between

(a) 25th January and 15th February

(b) 30th October and 11th December?

6 How many **days** are there from

(a) 27th March until 5th April

(b) 27th November until 25th December?

1 Write each time. Use am or pm.

(a)

Half past two

(b)

Quarter to eleven

(c)

Seven o'clock

(d) 25 minutes past 12 in the afternoon

(e) 10 minutes to 9 in the morning

(f) 5 minutes past 10 in the morning

(g) 20 minutes to 8 in the evening

2 Write these times in order.

(a) Start with the earliest morning time.

(b) Start with the latest evening time.

(c) Start with the earliest time.

    6.15 pm   9.35 am   5.25 am   3.45 pm

3 Write each time in a different way.

(a) 15 minutes to 8 in the morning   (b) 1.40 am

(c) 20 minutes past 12 in the evening   (d) 5.15 pm

I Write these times.

(a)

(b)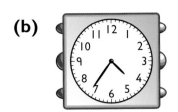

(c)

(d)

(e)

(f)

(g) quarter to 6   (h) 12 minutes past 9   (i) 18 minutes to 2

2  ⟶  26 minutes to 7.

Write these times.

(a)

(b)

(c)

(d)

(e)

(f)

3 Write these times in order.

(a) Start with the latest time.

(b) Start with the earliest time.

1 Write the time

(a) 50 minutes **after**

(b) 65 minutes after

(c) 1 hour and 30 minutes after

(d) 45 minutes after

(e) 70 minutes after

(f) 1 hour and 40 minutes after

(g) 55 minutes **before**

(h) 85 minutes before

(i) 1 hour and 50 minutes before

(j) 45 minutes before

(k) 95 minutes before

(l) 1 hour and 55 minutes before

2 How many minutes are there between each Start and Finish time?

Start   **Finish**   **Start**   **Finish**

(a)

(b)

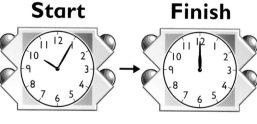

(c)

(d)

Times: five minute times past/to the hour, durations

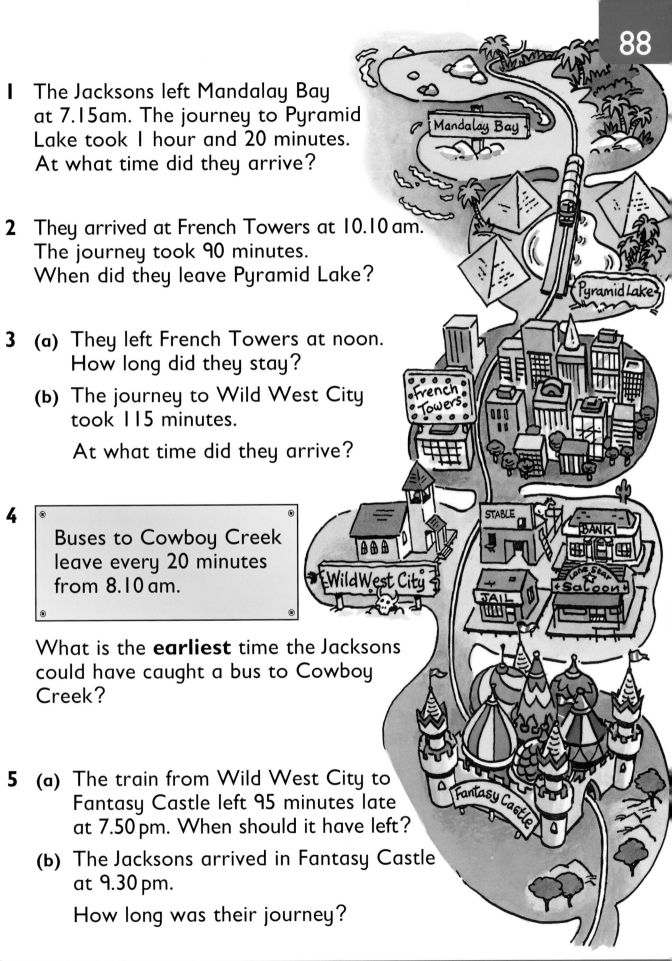

1 The Jacksons left Mandalay Bay at 7.15am. The journey to Pyramid Lake took 1 hour and 20 minutes. At what time did they arrive?

2 They arrived at French Towers at 10.10 am. The journey took 90 minutes. When did they leave Pyramid Lake?

3 (a) They left French Towers at noon. How long did they stay?

(b) The journey to Wild West City took 115 minutes.

At what time did they arrive?

4

Buses to Cowboy Creek leave every 20 minutes from 8.10 am.

What is the **earliest** time the Jacksons could have caught a bus to Cowboy Creek?

5 (a) The train from Wild West City to Fantasy Castle left 95 minutes late at 7.50 pm. When should it have left?

(b) The Jacksons arrived in Fantasy Castle at 9.30 pm.

How long was their journey?

Motorboat Timetable

	Morning	Afternoon
Balloch	depart 10.15	depart 3.35
Hayton	arr/dep 10.50	arr/dep (a)
Lowglen	arr/dep 11.10	arr/dep (b)
Deemouth	arrive 11.55	arrive (c)

1 How long does the motorboat take to sail
  (a) from Balloch to Hayton   **(b)** from Hayton to Lowglen
  (c) from Lowglen to Deemouth   **(d)** from Balloch to Deemouth?

2 At what time should the **afternoon** boat arrive at
  (a) Hayton   **(b)** Lowglen   **(c)** Deemouth?

3

Car Ferry to Benbray

Departs: 7.30 am 10.00 am
  12.30 pm 3.00 pm 5.30 pm

Sailing time: 25 minutes

How much time is there
(a) between ferries to Benbray
(b) between the first and last ferry?

4 What is the arrival time in Benbray of the ferry which
  (a) departs at 10.00 am   **(b)** departs at 5.30 pm?

5 How long does each person have to wait for a ferry?
  (a) Alana – arrives at 11.35 am   **(b)** Jason – arrives at 4.05 pm

6 The 12.30 pm ferry departs 40 minutes late.
  (a) At what time does it depart?
  (b) When does it arrive at Benbray?

Work with a partner.
You need cubes and a timer.

1 Find out how many times in **one minute** you can

    (a) write your name

    (b) touch your toes.

2 (a) How long do you **think** you would take to count out 100 cubes?

    (b) Use the timer to find out.

3 Which length of time is most likely to be correct?

    (a) Frying an egg takes ...

 ... about three minutes.   ... about thirty minutes.   ... about an hour.

    (b) You sleep at night for ...

... about five hours.   ... about fifteen hours.   ... about ten hours.

    (c) Walking across the playground takes ...

 ... about two seconds.   ... about twenty seconds.   ... about one hundred and twenty seconds.

4

 Summer lasts for three **months**.

Suggest something you would measure in

    (a) minutes   **(b)** seconds   **(c)** hours

    (d) weeks   **(e)** days   **(f)** years.

5 For how many months have you lived? Explain your answer.

Use a quarter-metre strip.

1 Measure these lengths. Label them as

| shorter than ¼ metre | **or** | longer than ¼ metre |

(a)

(b)

(c)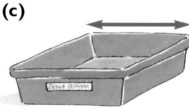

(d)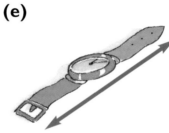

(e)

(f)

2 Find two objects
 (a) each about ¼ m long
 (b) longer than ¼ m but shorter than ½ m.

3 Which labels show the same height?

(a) 50 cm

(b) ¼ m

(c) 75 cm

(d) 1 m

(e) ¾ m

(f) 100 cm

(g) ½ m

(h) 25 cm

The board is 1 m 90 cm wide.

1 metre 90 centimetres

1 Estimate then measure

(a) the length of two desks

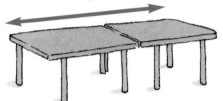

(b) your arm span

(c) the width of a bookcase

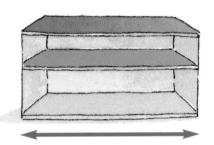

(d) the height of a door.

2 Write the missing heights.

Name	Height of sunflower		
Val	1 m 36 cm	136 cm	1·36 m
Jack	1 m 89 cm	**(a)**	1·89 m
Rosie	**(b)**	**(c)**	2·13 m
Josh	**(d)**	215 cm	**(e)**
Mo	2 m 8 cm	**(f)**	**(g)**
Kim	**(h)**	110 cm	**(i)**

3 Measure **(a)** your height **(b)** a friend's height.

Record each height in three different ways.

1 Who has given the best answer?

(a) | The height of a giraffe |

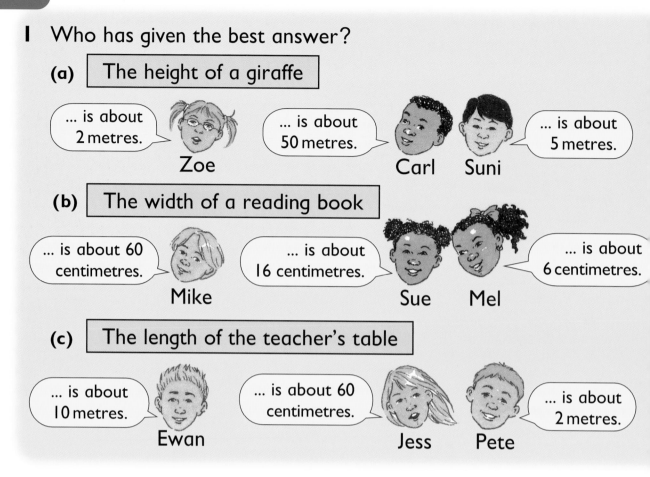

... is about 2 metres. — Zoe

... is about 50 metres. — Carl

... is about 5 metres. — Suni

(b) | The width of a reading book |

... is about 60 centimetres. — Mike

... is about 16 centimetres. — Sue

... is about 6 centimetres. — Mel

(c) | The length of the teacher's table |

... is about 10 metres. — Ewan

... is about 60 centimetres. — Jess

... is about 2 metres. — Pete

2 Which of these

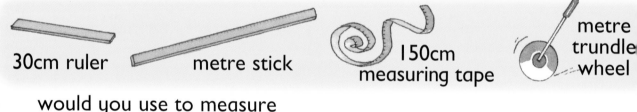

30cm ruler   metre stick   150cm measuring tape   metre trundle wheel

would you use to measure

(a) your height   **(b)** the length of a screw

(c) the length of the school hall

(d) the length of a pencil

(e) the distance around a basketball

(f) the width of a football pitch

(g) the distance around a tree trunk?

3 List four other things you would measure in

(a) centimetres   **(b)** metres.

1 Find the perimeter of each shape in metres, by **counting**.

(a)

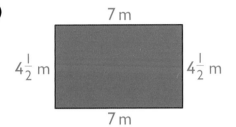

7 m

$4\frac{1}{2}$ m $4\frac{1}{2}$ m

7 m

(b)

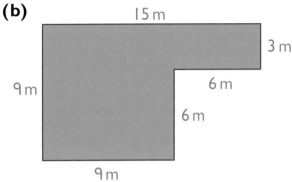

15 m

3 m

9 m   6 m

6 m

9 m

2 Find the perimeter of each shape in centimetres, by **measuring**.

(a)

(b)

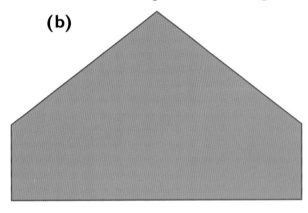

(c)

(d)

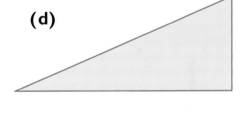

3 Measure the perimeter of

(a) your maths textbook
(b) a computer screen
(c) your classroom
(d) a gym mat.

4 (a) Draw a shape with a perimeter of 20 cm.

(b) Draw two **different** rectangles each with a perimeter of 12 cm.

melon 800 g

banana 150 g

apple 500 g

pumpkin 1000 g

yam 750 g

lemon 250 g

cucumber 700 g

orange 300 g

1 Which items weigh

(a) more than $\frac{1}{2}$ kg

(b) less than $\frac{1}{2}$ kg

(c) less than $\frac{1}{4}$ kg

(d) more than $\frac{3}{4}$ kg

(e) more than $\frac{1}{2}$ kg and less than $\frac{3}{4}$ kg

(f) more than $\frac{1}{4}$ kg and less than $\frac{1}{2}$ kg

(g) between $\frac{3}{4}$ kg and 1 kg?

2 List **two** items which together weigh

(a) $\frac{3}{4}$ kg

(b) $1\frac{1}{4}$ kg

(c) $1\frac{1}{2}$ kg

(d) 1 kg?

3 List **three** items which together weigh $1\frac{1}{2}$ kg?

4 How many more grams should be added to make

(a) $\frac{1}{2}$ kg

(b) $\frac{1}{4}$ kg

(c) $\frac{3}{4}$ kg

(d) 1 kg?

270 g 190 g 450 g 380 g

5 Write in order, starting with the lightest weight.

| 550 g | $\frac{1}{4}$ kg | $\frac{3}{4}$ kg | 200 g | $\frac{1}{2}$ kg | 1000 g | 700 g |

1 Write in order

(a) starting with the **lightest** weight

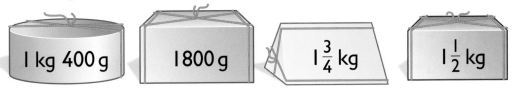

(b) starting with the **heaviest** weight.

2 Write in **grams**.

(a) 1 kg 650 g **(b)** 3 kg 485 g **(c)** 2 kg 193 g **(d)** 2 kg 95 g

3 Write in **kilograms and grams**.

(a) 2222 g **(b)** 1906 g **(c)** 1100 g **(d)** 3070 g

4 Write the total weight in **kg and g** of the tins on each tray.

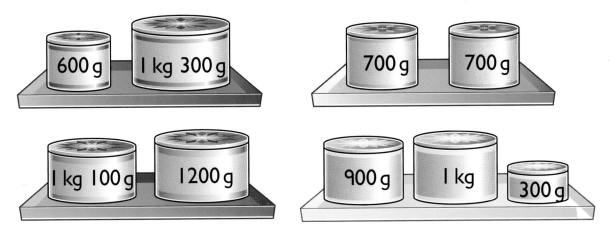

5 Which trays have tins which together weigh

(a) more than $1\frac{3}{4}$ kg **(b)** less than 2000 g?

1 Use  .

How many

(a) pencils altogether weigh about 50 g

(b) exercise books altogether weigh about 200 g?

2 Find something that weighs between 150 g and 250 g.

3 The box weighs less than 800 g.

Write about the weight of each of these items.

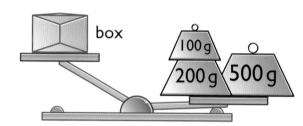

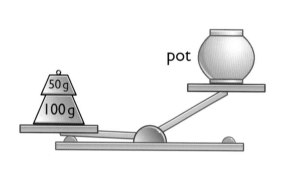

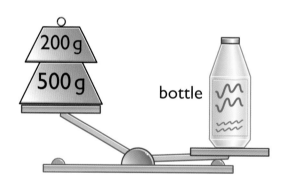

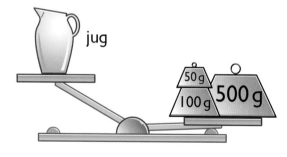

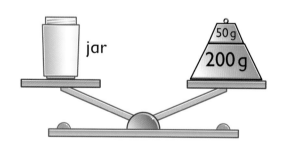

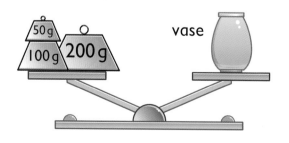

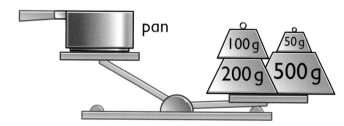

Weight: 50 g, 100 g, 200 g, 500 g weights

1 Beth has some 500 g, 200 g, 100 g and 50 g weights.

List the weights she could use to balance each item.

Use as few weights as possible.

(a)

300 g

(b)

450 g

(c)

1600 g

(d)

1 kg 250 g

2 Find the weight of

(a) the box

200 g

500 g

(b) the tin

50 g
100 g

50 g

(c) the bottle

50 g
100 g

200 g

(d) the jar.

100 g
500 g

50 g
200 g

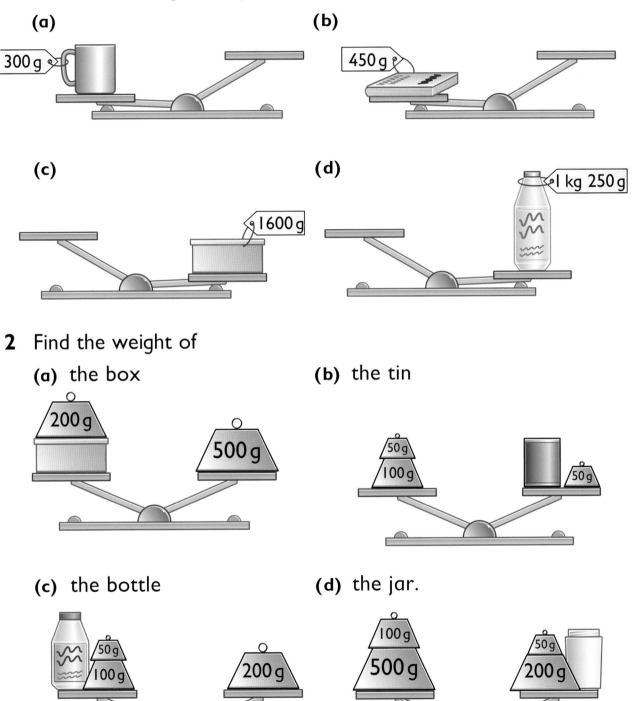

1 Find each area in **square centimetres.**

(a)   (b)

(c)   (d)

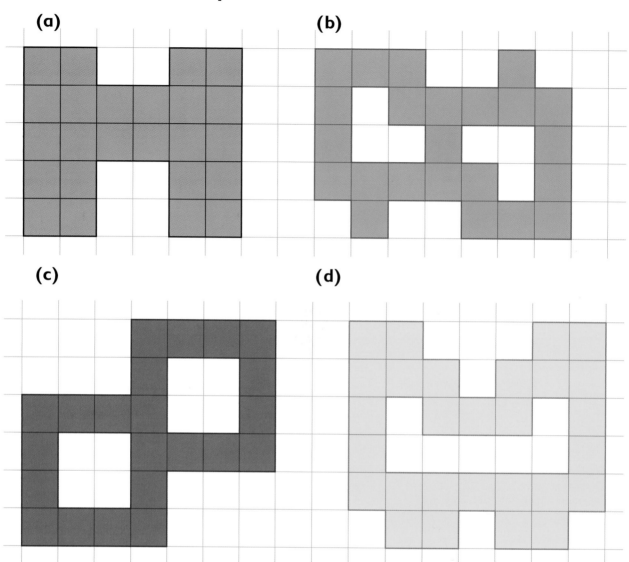

2 Which two shapes have a total area of

(a) 15 cm²   (b) 18 cm²   (c) 17 cm² ?

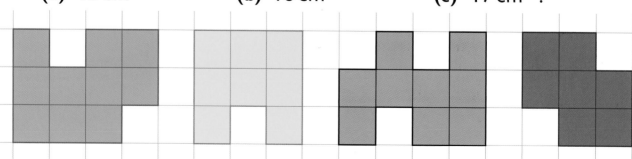

3 Draw three rectangles each with an area of 24 cm².

1 Which shapes have an area of 2cm²?

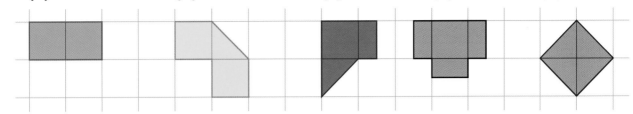

(a) (b) (c) (d) (e)

2 Find the area of each shape in **square centimetres.**

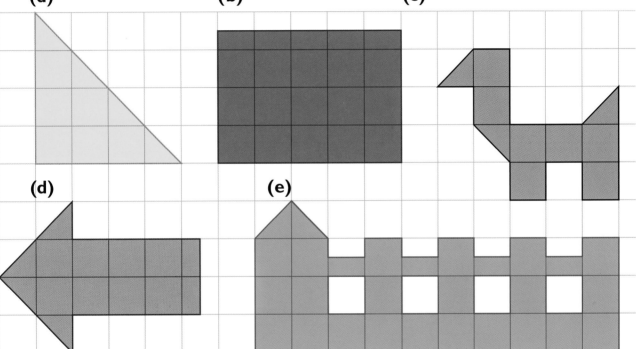

(a) (b) (c)

(d) (e)

3 (a) Draw a shape with an area of $7\frac{1}{2}$ cm².

(b) Draw three different shapes each with an area of $5\frac{1}{2}$ cm².

4 Find different ways of colouring **half** the area of a square like this.

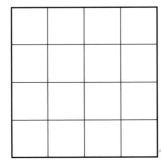

101

Use water or sand, a and a  1 litre $\frac{1}{2}$ litre

1 You need containers like these.

Find to the nearest half-litre the amount of sand or water each container holds.

LEMON 250 ml APPLE 750 ml STRAWBERRY 900 ml PEAR 800 ml PEACH 400 ml PLUM 200 ml ORANGE 600 ml GRAPE 500 ml

2 Which juice containers hold
  (a) more than $\frac{1}{2}\ell$ (b) less than $\frac{1}{2}\ell$ (c) less than $\frac{1}{4}\ell$
  (d) more than $\frac{3}{4}\ell$ (e) between $\frac{1}{4}\ell$ and $\frac{3}{4}\ell$
  (f) more than $\frac{1}{2}\ell$ and less than $\frac{3}{4}\ell$?

3 List **two** containers which together hold
  (a) 1 ℓ (b) $\frac{3}{4}\ell$ (c) $1\frac{1}{4}\ell$ (d) $1\frac{1}{2}\ell$.

4 List **three** containers which together hold $1\frac{1}{4}$ litres.

5 Write in order, starting with the smallest amount.

| $\frac{3}{4}\ell$ | 1001 ml | $\frac{1}{2}\ell$ | 300 ml | $\frac{1}{4}\ell$ | 850 ml | 1 ℓ |

Capacity: litres/mililitres, relationships

1 Write each missing amount from the table.

Name	Amount	
Katy	2ℓ 500 ml	2500 ml
Max	1ℓ 200 ml	**(a)**
Lucy	**(b)**	3700 ml
Colin	**(c)**	**(d)**
Mia	**(e)**	**(f)**

2 Write in millilitres.

(a) 2ℓ 450 ml   (b) 1ℓ 710 ml   (c) 3ℓ 805 ml   (d) 1ℓ 25 ml

3 Write in litres and millilitres.

(a) 1760 ml   (b) 3333 ml   (c) 4308 ml   (d) 2050 ml

4

How many of each container can be filled from the 1 litre barrel?

You need 3D shapes like these.

1 Match each shape to its name.

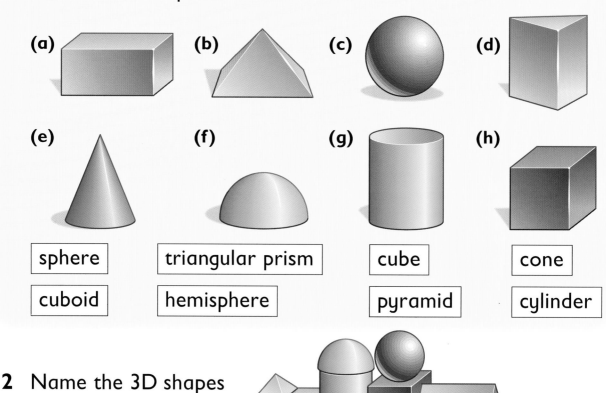

sphere | triangular prism | cube | cone

cuboid | hemisphere | pyramid | cylinder

2 Name the 3D shapes in this model.

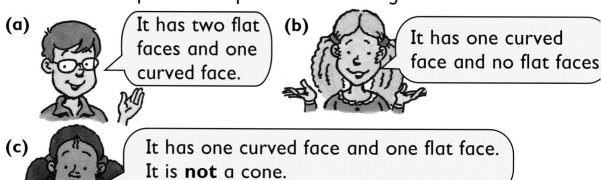

3 (a) Build your own model using 3D shapes.

(b) Name the shapes you used.

4 Which 3D shape is each person describing?

(a) It has two flat faces and one curved face.

(b) It has one curved face and no flat faces

(c) It has one curved face and one flat face. It is **not** a cone.

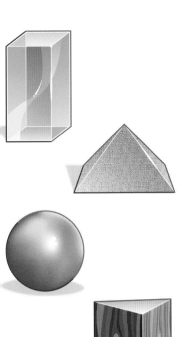

1 How many vertices does each shape have?

cuboid ➞ 8 vertices

2 Which shape has 1 vertex?

3 Which shapes have

(a) 6 vertices   (b) no vertices

(c) the same number of vertices?

4 (a) Count and record the number of **straight** edges for each shape.

cuboid ➞ 12 edges

(b) Which shapes have the same number of straight edges?

5 Which shapes have curved edges?

6 Look at these pairs of shapes.

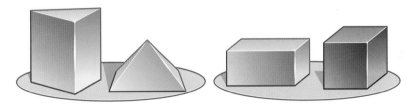

(a) What is the **same** about the shapes in each pair?

(b) What is different about them?

7 Write clues to describe this shape.

Cube

1 Use flat shapes to build

(a) a cuboid

(b) a triangular prism

(c) a square-based pyramid.

2 Use straws and joiners to build

(a) a cube

(b) a triangular-based pyramid

(c) a hexagonal prism.

3

(a) Choose a carton.
Cut along edges using scissors
then unfold to make a net.

(b) Would this net make a cube?
Find out by joining squares.

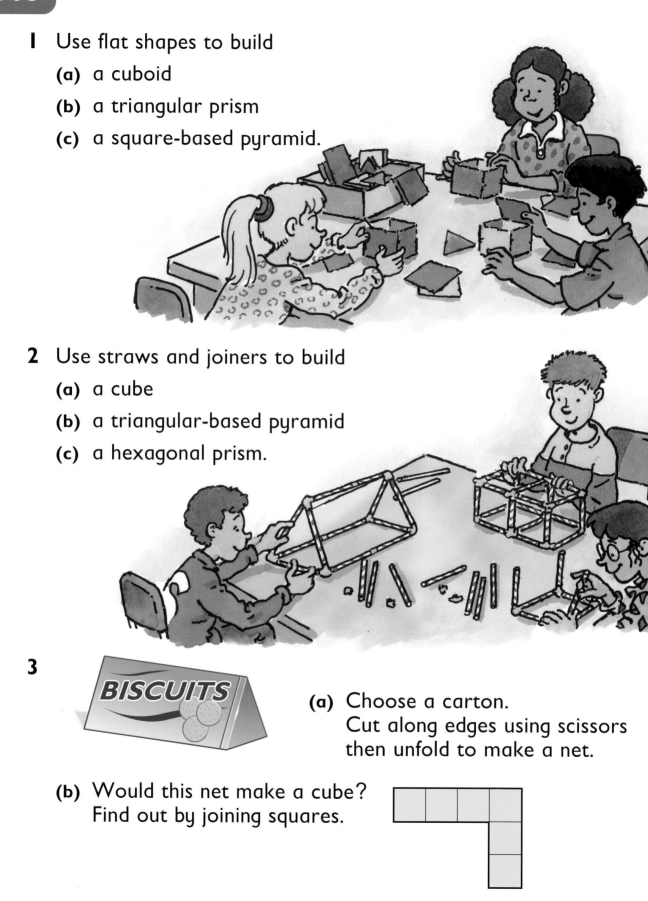

Use linking cubes.

1 Build each shape.

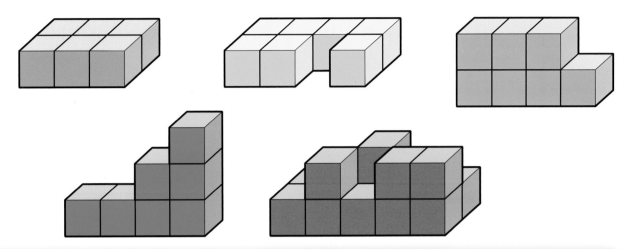

2 (a) How many cubes do you **think** are needed to build each of these shapes?

(b) Check by building each shape.

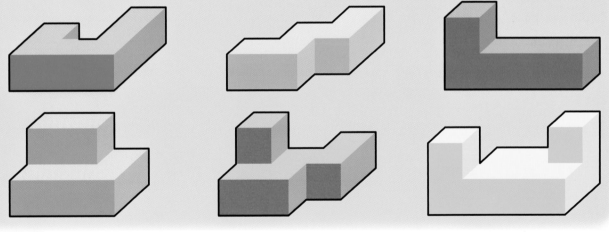

3 Build as many **different** cuboids as you can using

(a) 12 cubes

(b) 24 cubes.

All of the sides are of equal length.

Brad

Only two angles are equal.

Jenny

1 Who is describing

(a) an isosceles triangle

(b) an equilateral triangle?

2 Which of these shapes are

• equilateral triangles

• isosceles triangles?

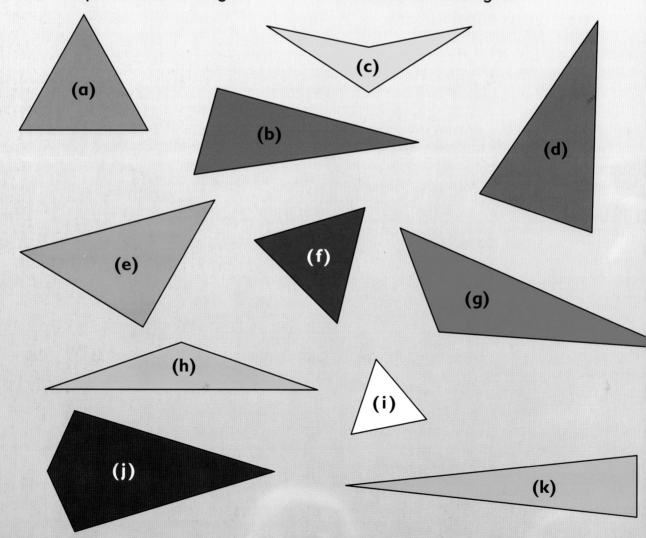

(a)

(b)

(c)

(d)

(e)

(f)

(g)

(h)

(i)

(j)

(k)

1 Which of these coloured shapes

   (a) are quadrilaterals   **(b)** are triangles   **(c)** are regular

   (d) have a right angle   **(e)** have fewer than four angles

   (f) have more than six sides?

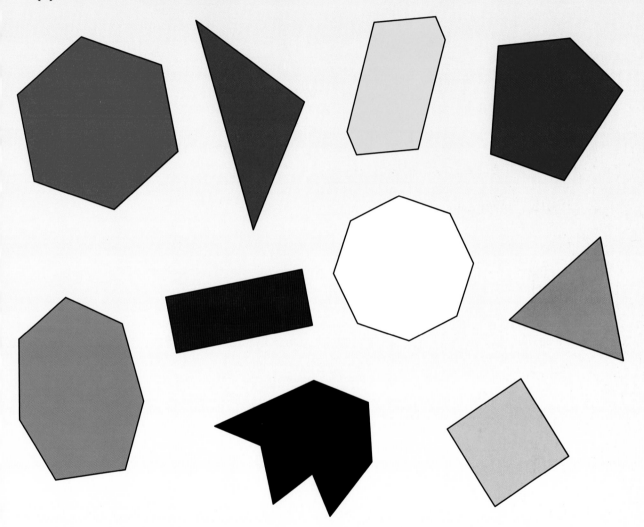

2 What colour is

   (a) the **isosceles** triangle   **(b)** the **regular** hexagon

   (c) the **irregular** octagon   **(d)** the heptagon?

3 Name the shape which is coloured

   (a) purple   **(b)** yellow   **(c)** orange.

1 Use two **isosceles** triangles to make each of these shapes.

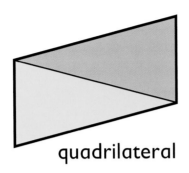

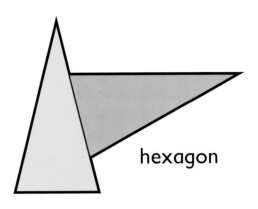

quadrilateral

hexagon

2 Use the two isosceles triangles. Make then draw

(a) a pentagon   (b) a **different** hexagon

(c) **two** different quadrilaterals.

3 Use dotty paper. Copy and continue each pattern of triangles.

1 How many lines of symmetry does each **shape** have?

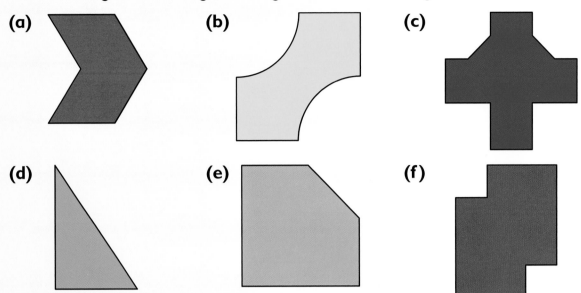

(a)

(b)

(c)

(d)

(e)

(f)

2 Sketch a shape with

(a) **only** one line of symmetry   (b) **only** two lines of symmetry.

3 How many lines of symmetry does each **design** have?

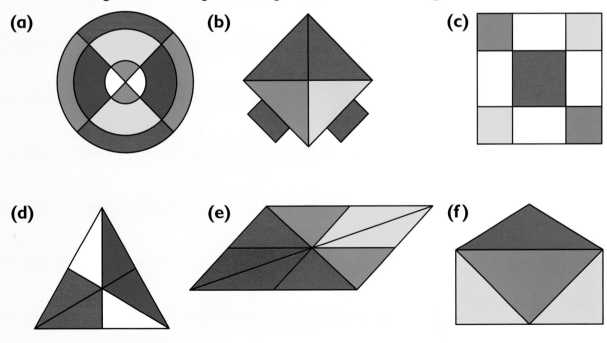

(a)

(b)

(c)

(d)

(e)

(f)

Use squared paper.

1 Copy and colour to make each pattern symmetrical.

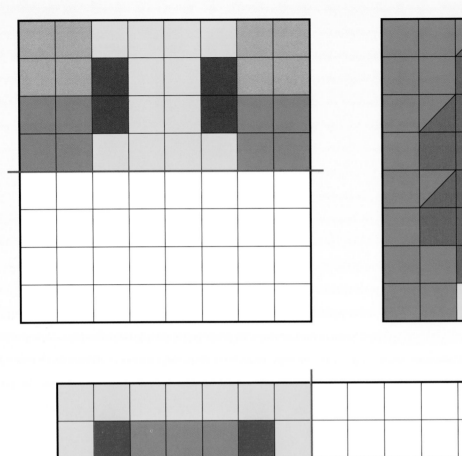

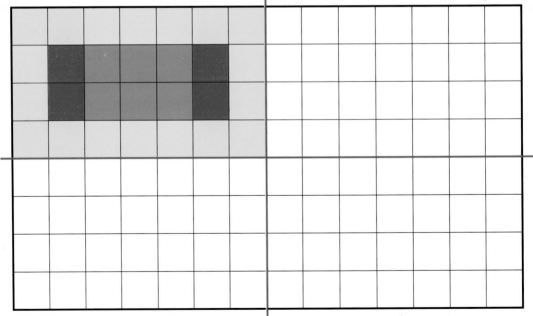

2 Make **part** of a symmetrical pattern for a friend to complete.
Draw the line of symmetry.

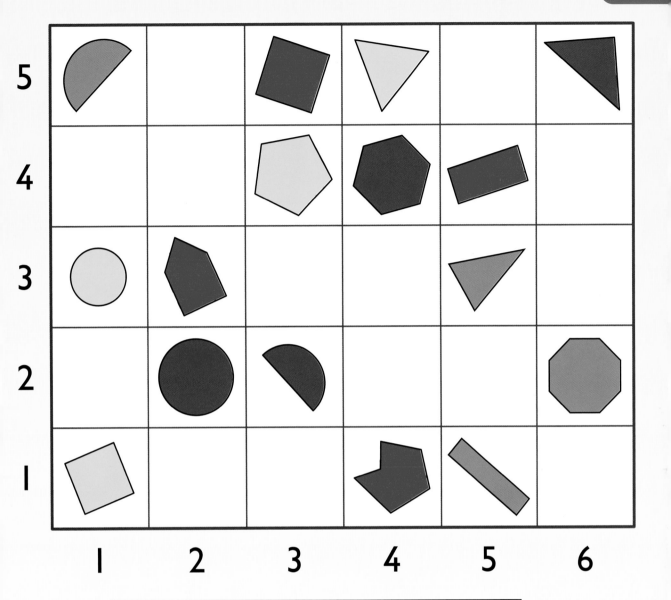

The **red square** is at position **3,5**

The **green triangle** is at position **5,3**.

1 At what position is the

(a) blue triangle   (b) yellow square   (c) blue hexagon

(d) red pentagon   (e) red hexagon   (f) green octagon?

2 What is at position

(a) 2,2   (b) 3,4   (c) 1,5   (d) 5,4   (e) 4,5 ?

1 The red dot has co-ordinates (0,2).

What are the co-ordinates of the

(a) orange dot

(b) white dot

(c) blue dot

(d) black dot

(e) yellow dot

(f) green dot

(g) purple dot

(h) brown dot?

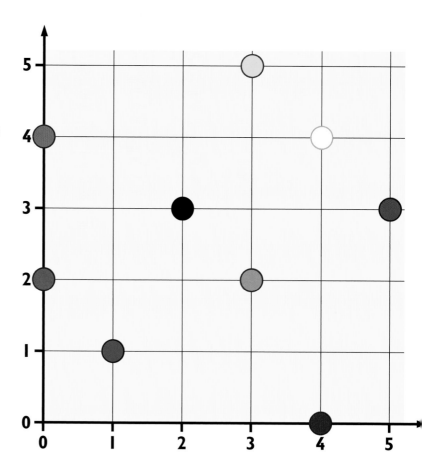

2 What colour is the dot at each of these positions?

(a) (1,2) **(b)** (6,1) **(c)** (2,1) **(d)** (5,0) **(e)** (8,2)

(f) (7,0) **(g)** (3,3) **(h)** (2,2) **(i)** (0,3)

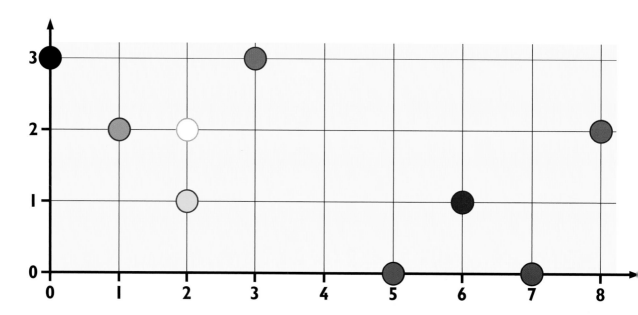

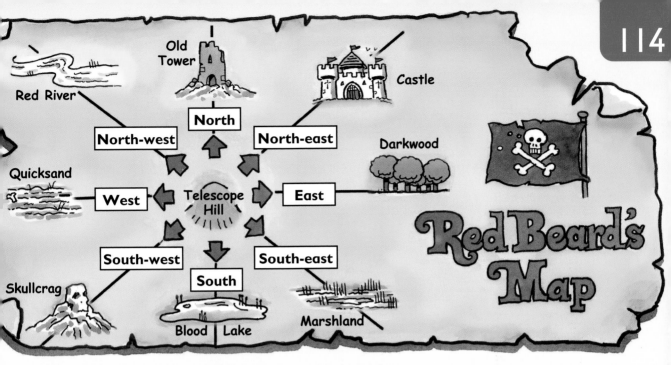

You are on top of Telescope Hill.

1 What do you see when you look

(a) North (b) South-west (c) East (d) North-east?

2 In which direction is

(a) Blood Lake (b) Red River (c) Quicksand (d) Marshland?

3 Face East.

What do you see when you turn through

(a) a half turn (b) a right angle anti-clockwise (c) a whole turn?

4 Face North-west.

In which direction are you facing when you turn through

(a) a quarter turn clockwise (b) 3 right angles clockwise?

5 Describe these turns.

(a) Face Skullcrag. Turn to face Red River.

(b) Face Blood Lake. Turn to face Darkwood.

(c) Face Red River. Turn to face the Marshland.

The towers in Redbeard's castle are linked by tunnels.

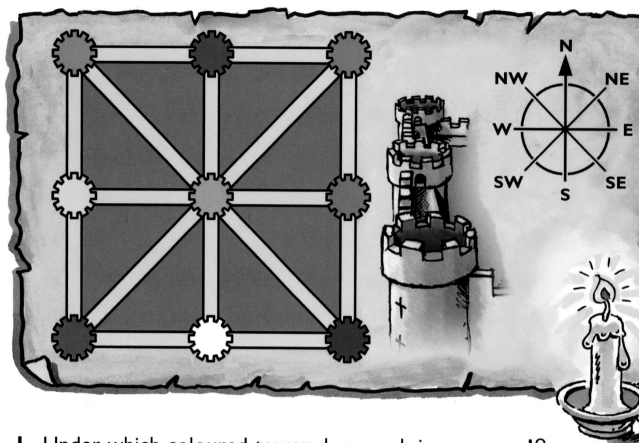

I Under which coloured tower does each journey **end**?

   (a) Start at 🔘 . Go through 1 tunnel North-east,
   2 tunnels West and 1 tunnel South.

   (b) Start at 🔘 . Go through 1 tunnel South, 2 tunnels North-west
   and 2 tunnels East.

2 **Describe a route**

   (a) from 🔘 to 🔘 that does **not** pass through 🔘

   (b) from 🔘 to 🔘 that does not pass through 🔘 **or** 🔘

   (c) from 🔘 to 🔘 that passes through 🔘 , 🔘 **and** 🔘 .

3 Describe two **different** routes from 🔘 to 🔘 .

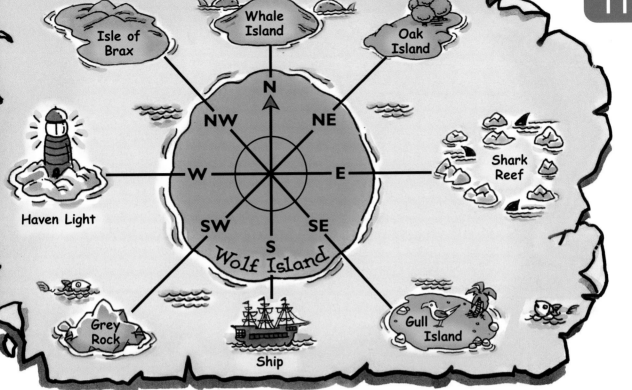

You are at the centre of Wolf Island.

1 **Face North**.
   In which direction are you facing after you turn through

   (a) 90° anti-clockwise   (b) 180° clockwise

   (c) 45° clockwise   (d) 360° anti-clockwise?

2 **Face South-east**.
   What do you see after you turn through

   (a) 90° clockwise   (b) 45° anti-clockwise

   (c) 180° anti-clockwise   (d) 45° clockwise?

3 Describe each turn.

   (a) Face Gull Island. Turn to face Oak Island.

   (b) Face Grey Rock. Turn to face Haven Light.

   (c) Face Isle of Brax. Turn to face Gull Island.

   (d) Face Oak Island. Turn to face Whale Island.

1   The spokes on the ship's wheel are each 30° apart.
    Use the letters to find the treasure.

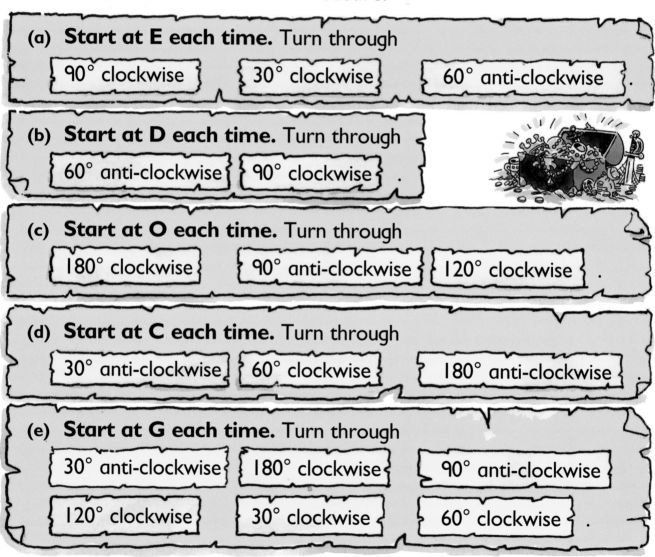

(a) **Start at E each time.** Turn through

   | 90° clockwise | | 30° clockwise | | 60° anti-clockwise | .

(b) **Start at D each time.** Turn through

   | 60° anti-clockwise | 90° clockwise | .

(c) **Start at O each time.** Turn through

   | 180° clockwise | | 90° anti-clockwise | 120° clockwise | .

(d) **Start at C each time.** Turn through

   | 30° anti-clockwise | 60° clockwise | | 180° anti-clockwise | .

(e) **Start at G each time.** Turn through

   | 30° anti-clockwise | 180° clockwise | | 90° anti-clockwise |

   | 120° clockwise | 30° clockwise | | 60° clockwise | .

2   **Start at C each time.**
    Write turns to make the word **GOLD**.

FALCON PARK

OPEN: April to September
9.00 am – 6.00 pm
ENTRY: Adult £5 Child £3·50

Special Events	Date	Location
Go-carts	Sat 29 July	Race Track
Insect World	Sat 5 August	Green Tent
Hot Wheels	Sat 12 August	Race Track
Tree Trail	Sat 19 August	Old Tower
Discovery Day	Sat 26 August	Science Dome
Bumpers	Sat 2 September	Race Track

1 For how many months of the year is Falcon Park open?

2 For how many hours is Falcon Park open each day?

3 Which events take place at the Race Track?

4 Which event will take place on **(a)** 5 Aug **(b)** 26 Aug?

5 What is the total cost of a day at Falcon Park for 2 adults and 4 children?

6 Which events do you think are held indoors?

SESSION STARTS AT	Number of visitors			
	9.00 am	10.30 am	12.00 noon	1.30 pm
Forest Trek	12	18	9	19
River Raft	13	27	11	29
Megawall	15	17	13	20
Archery	6	19	15	15

7 Which event had most visitors over the whole day?

8 How many visitors in total attended the 1.30 pm sessions?

9 Find the event **and** when it started, which had
 (a) most visitors **(b)** fewest visitors?

10 Did more people go to morning or afternoon events? Explain.

Insects seen at Falcon Park   Total

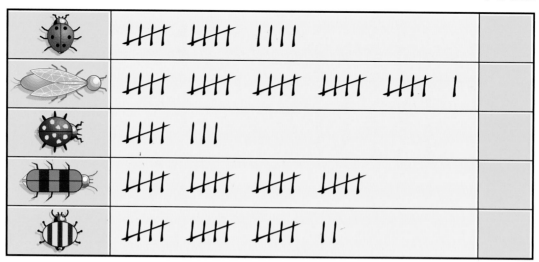

1 How many of each kind of insect were seen?

(a)   (b)  (c)   (d)   (e)

2 How many insects altogether were seen?

3 How many insects had (a) spots (b) stripes?

4 How many more insects were

(a) than   (b) than ?

When insects were seen   Total

Time	Tally	Total
10.00 am – 10.15 am	ЖЖ ЖЖ ‖	
11.30 am – 11.45 am	ЖЖ ЖЖ ЖЖ ‖	
1.15 pm – 1.30 pm	ЖЖ ЖЖ ЖЖ ЖЖ ‖	
2.45 pm – 3.00 pm	ЖЖ ЖЖ ЖЖ ЖЖ ЖЖ ЖЖ ‖‖	

5 How many insects were seen at
(a) 10.00 am – 10.15 am   (b) 11.30 am – 11.45 am
(c) 1.15 pm – 1.30 pm   (d) 2.45 pm – 3.00 pm?

6 Was the morning or the afternoon the better time to see insects? Explain.

Year 4 Holiday Survey

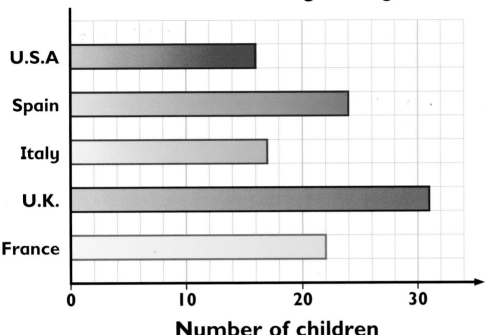

Number of children

I Which country was visited by

   (a) the greatest number of children

   (b) the smallest number of children.

2 Which was the third most visited country?

3 How many children took holidays

   (a) abroad   **(b)** in **another** European country?

4 How many more children had a holiday

   (a) in the U.K. than in France   **(b)** in Spain than in the U.S.A?

5 How many Year 4 children altogether had a holiday?

6 Which two countries together were visited by a total of thirty-three Year 4 children?

Class 4 pets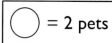

1 Which pet is

(a) most common

(b) least common?

2 How many more pets are

(a) dogs than cats

(b) fish than birds?

Number of pets

3 How many pets do Class 4 children have altogether?

4 How many Class 4 pets have more than two legs?

dog cat bird fish

Tropical fish tank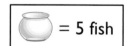

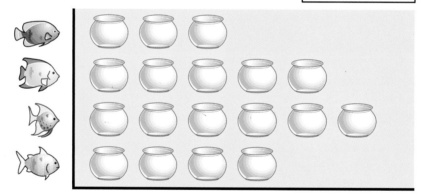

Number of fish

5 How many fish are (a) (b) (c) (d) ?

6 How many fish altogether are in the tank?

7 How many more fish are

(a) than (b) than (c) than ?

1 (a) Write the letters in a diagram like this.

Has a line of symmetry	~~Has a line of symmetry~~

(b) Choose four more letters. Write them in the diagram.

2 (a) Write the Gang's names in a diagram like this.

	glasses	~~glasses~~
beard		
~~beard~~		

(b) Repeat for this diagram.

	hat	no hat
male		
not male		

The Grizzly Gang

Joe   Kay

Mike   Sally

Dave   Bill

Dot   Jim

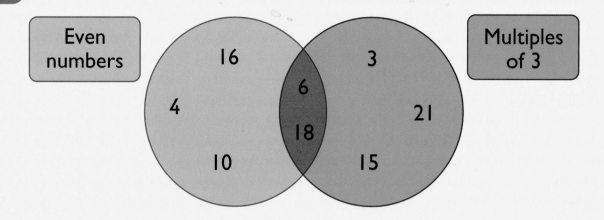

Even numbers

Multiples of 3

1 List three other numbers which could go in

(a) the green part   (b) the blue part   (c) the red part.

2 Where in the Venn diagram should each of these numbers go?

(a) 8   (b) 30   (c) 27   (d) 19

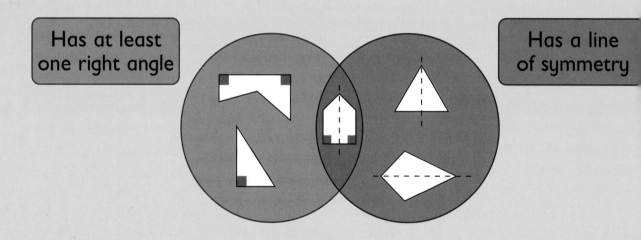

Has at least one right angle

Has a line of symmetry

3 In which part of the Venn diagram should each of these shapes go?

(a)   (b)

4 Use squared paper. Draw a shape which could go in

(a) the orange part (b) the purple part (c) the brown part.